FACE to FACE

FACE to FACE

VOLUME ONE
Missing Love

MARTY FOLSOM

WIPF & STOCK · Eugene, Oregon

FACE TO FACE
Volume One: Missing Love

Scripture quotations taken from the New American Standard Bible®, Copyright © 1960, 1962, 1963, 1968, 1971, 1972, 1973, 1975, 1977, 1995 by The Lockman Foundation. Used by permission.

Wipf & Stock
An Imprint of Wipf and Stock Publishers
199 W. 8th Ave., Suite 3
Eugene, OR 97401

www.wipfandstock.com

ISBN 13: 978-1-62564-096-3

Manufactured in the U.S.A.

Dedicated to
Lucinda M. Folsom
My beloved wife, patron saint, and dearest companion

Contents

Preface

THIS BOOK WAS BORN out of years of people asking me to write down a theology that they could continue to savor, like the theology I passionately present: a theology that enriches daily life in our cherished relationships. One day, a personal coach suggested that I write about loving and being loved, since he had heard that as a constant theme in my life. I took that seed, and let it grow. The work that you are about to read combines my discovery process with the insights of great minds that have influenced my world. These pages create a woven-together tapestry that illustrates personal relationships. The life of this book draws from the deep wells of theology, philosophy, and therapy, not abstractly, but in the "ah-ha" moments, where the clouds parted and I could see the logic of love in practice. It tells a narrative theology that echoes ancient texts, like singing an ancient score in a new arrangement. I love that stories sing meaning into our lives, and braid our identity as they enable us to find our place within our families, communities, and most intimate personal relations; this is our most profound and primal education.

The original form of this book required an Olympic level of endurance to complete the race, so I decided to extend grace to my readers and gather around three focal points. This text in your hands is the first of three volumes that will investigate, in unique ways, the nature of personal relationships. This initial volume takes on the challenges we encounter in relating to God and our fellow-humans. It is a hopeful diagnosis that opens doors to understand why we are so fractured, frustrated, and fear-based, in ways that sabotage our lives, rather than giving us the life we were created to experience. In the second book, we will explore the nature of personal relating from the richest resources of theology, philosophy, and therapy. It will not be a self-help book, but rather an Einsteinian shift in how we think about being persons in relation. In the third volume, we will explore and expand the mystery of what we mean when talking about our desire to truly relate to and serve God as kingdom-of-God people.

I was nudged into this writing process. A creative collaborator in my life, Scott Burnett, inspired the style of this book when he introduced me to creative nonfiction. I entered the genre through Anne Lamott's work, and loved her life-wise ways of revealing her struggles and joys. Her witty authenticity got into my blood. Don Miller's *Blue Like Jazz* further inclined me to use story to allow theology to speak, even to those who are not theologically trained.

I find joy in making space for the human search for the meaning of existence in its fullest bloom. We theologians are on the threatened species list because we often fail to engage the people we hope to enlighten, in terms they understand. The style of the book's words may not always fit with how you are feeling each day, but if you return often and share your discoveries with others, the insights may grow in satisfaction. Most of us are missing vocabulary to engage our relationship with God. Relating to God seems so vague and distant, but it need not be that way.

While there may be nothing new under the sun, we may need to take off our sunglasses to see new colors. What a different experience it is to see a Van Gogh picture in a book, flat on the page, versus standing in front of an original to feel its movement. Being present to the reality is life transforming. This book is like a kaleidoscope that takes broken pieces from life's journey (my story), shines a common light (God's story), and enables you to move with it to see beauty for you alone (your story). I hope you find yourself visiting deep, hidden inklings you have pondered. This book requires an honest look at the challenges that confront our relationships, and the sources of the breakdowns. The discussions will bring to light constructive understanding, and reveal the inadequacy of old patterns. Turning up the soil makes ready opportunity for new growth.

It was a profound moment for me when my wife, who is a dentist, taught me that the PhDs in dentistry are teachers and researchers who study the tools and premises that challenge hands-on doctors as they consider the patient in the chair. Thus, dentistry's scholars serve doctors in practical ways. I believe theology needs the same kind of connection between learning institutions and practical applications. Good theology heals broken lives and communities. This book explores bringing together the worlds of learning and living to find new ways forward.

I serve as a bridge person between isolated people who need to be in dialog: church and academy, theologians and everyday people, and theology and therapy. This book reflects those diverse islands of interest. I pray you find yourself island-hopping with a spirit of adventure that transforms your relationships and opens a fulfilled life.

Many seekers of truth ask big questions about the presence of evil in the world: How can God exist when there is so much bad news? But I am more deeply concerned with the absence of love in our lives. This is the epidemic of our times. We are relationally ignorant. There is anguish in the search for love, and gradual numbness for those exhausted by the quest for meaningful connection.

If you are not a Christian and are reading this book, you may not identify with some of what I say in these pages. But I, too, would probably reject the version of Christianity you resist because it is too judgmental, "in the head," or has a distant or angry God. Keep reading to see that a whole new world is possible. If you are a Christian, you may find that my presentation is not like what you have experienced before. I emphasize the personal nature of God, who intends to restore relationships and persons, rather than a God who requires a specific rational belief or conformity to a set of rules. Keep reading to see the face and hear the voice of God.

The expression "face-to-face" images a personal relationship. Such a fulfilling closeness is my goal for you. This head-on phrase may depict the experience of a long-awaited and passionately-satisfying kiss. Negatively, it may bring the picture of an intense confrontation between two embarrassingly-immature should-be-adults bumping enraged noses. The expansive spectrum between these contrasting images is where most of us reside. Many of us desire to regularly enjoy good face-to-face interactions with family and friends. Some wish to experience this engagement with God, like Moses, who knew God face-to-face as a friend. However, this seems crazy-impossible. God is too distant, and we are too busy, enslaved by our to-do lists. Life is often a lonely and exhausting endurance race. Love struggles to bloom like some lonely wildflower in the cracks.

I contrast personal with impersonal relationships. Most of our relating is impersonal, even with family. Just because we share space with other humans does not mean we know one another. We are immersed in a sea of humanity that washes over us like waves. Those are impersonal relations. But persons who enter like fresh, crisp water into our lives are the ones that sustain and nourish our personal existence. They bring love and acceptance like vitamins, and challenges like sandpaper to polish. These people achieve the personal level; they are rare frontiers worth exploring.

Problems within relationships are immense. The biggest part of the human relations pie chart is populated with the fallen-out-of-love, many even while still married. I, too, have wrestled with face-to-face love all my life. Like Jacob, who was renamed Israel (he wrestles with God), I wear both scars and promises as well. These signs provide a warp and woof for inquiry into the possibility of both understanding and experiencing rich relating.

I have discovered forgotten ways and new tools to take on this most important of life's issues: engaging in meaningful relationships. Most people lack the elemental tools of relating, and skills to use them. We are not taught these most basic life-skills in school. Maybe I missed that day in class. I find the absence epidemic in Western culture. There lives a silence in so many human souls, a cancerous vacuum. We need life practices that rehabilitate us. Like caring for our teeth, relational skills are not difficult. However, engaging in meaningful relationships requires others who actually employ these skills with us until they become embedded in us.

Our families grew up in a culturally supported Age of Roles and Rules. That age is passing. In its place is a new playing field where we might, with some coaching, enter an Age of Relating. Like the sailor in the crow's-nest, we see it from a distance. I cannot take you to this place, but I can show you how to build that ship.

Introduction

ONE MIGHT BE TEMPTED to think of the chapters of this volume as merely memoirs from the life of a theologian, but that assumption would miss their vision. Rather, they are reflections on illuminating stories that make theology visible in everyday life. They play out in narrative form, rather than in traditional, rational arguments that feel so black and white when set next to the textured strokes that paint our lives each day with messy colors. This is a book of serious theology for those who wish to take back roads to bathe in beauty or adventure. These travelers may eventually end up with dear friends at their desired journey's end. But many get lost along the way, or wonder how to start the journey. This book highlights what is missing in our lives, what keeps us from experiencing a face-to-face relationship with the triune God. Each vista opens to give us a glimpse of the glory of meaningful personal relating.

This is a textbook, exploring theology for both premodern and postmodern thinkers. In its pursuit of knowledge, the passing modern world made humanity its central focus. When doing theology, it attempted to give proofs, arguments, definitions, and an organization to human knowledge about God that felt impersonal and abstract. Most publishers still prefer books that are logical, argue a point, and add to the human conversation about God. Poets and storytellers are kindly exited.

The premodern world focused on the stories of peoples who rehearsed history to remember where they came from. Thus, they practiced traditions to celebrate their unique and often painful past. Their culture joined them together through a common narrative. This usually included God as the source of meaning and direction. The Bible is a premodern book. It invites us to live within its story, revealing the God who enters our human drama in order to overcome separation. In much the same way, this book uses story to teach us to discover ourselves as those being drawn into the biblical story, but not by merely defining points of doctrine. This book departs from being premodern by using contemporary concepts, at that time undiscovered, to uncover what is missing in the face-to-face relationships the Bible envisions: "Now I know in part, but then I shall see face-to-face" (1 Corinthians 13:12, paraphrased).

Many may not know the term "postmodern." It refers to a way of thinking that no longer lets humans arrogantly define reality and manage a power struggle, trying to get the world into "order." Postmodernity is a protest against modernity. Modern thinking tries to regulate the world by developing a body of scientific knowledge. This reduces the known creation to manageable words and ideas through which humans control the world. During the 1960s, many resisted "the Man," and yearned to find a more humane journey. That desire was a postmodern reaction. But positively, postmodern explorers search for the possibility of retooling our use of words and conversations to connect with God and one another, rather than understanding knowledge as a box of categories neatly labeled. I am one of those explorers.

There is a deep longing in many of us to live with a sense of mystery, and to enter into meaning, by hearing stories.

Storytelling is the heartbeat of a postmodern. The imagination takes us to an understanding that is unavailable to mechanistic science, which excludes discussing persons or God. The thirst for a meaningful life is still alive, and calls for a paradigm shift from seeing the world as merely all about objects. Instead, the new perspective holds a vision of the world as personally interpreted. It is best inhabited by those who learn to relate respectfully to what is other than themselves, to actually "touch" the world, and be transformed in that encounter. This book, then, is an expression of theology that does not study God or the human in separate observations or laboratories. This book contributes to the study of theology by more appropriately allowing us to enter into the relationship "between us." From that vista point, we more adequately grasp who God is, who we are, and what is wrong. Thus, we begin to see the inviting path that prompts us to live a relational theology that restores persons in relationships as the Bible intends.

Chapter 1 introduces two struggles that are important in our time; the first is the nature of language as the tool of engaging reality: How do our words connect us to reality or what matters? Wittgenstein and others have invited us to move beyond dictionary definitions to recognize that we play a language game: always volleying words in ways that strike us uniquely as they move us in each new encounter. Life enhances when we pay attention to the specific meaning of the person in front of us, instead of the usual language sense that dictionaries and clinical studies try to achieve. Language is the toolbox of personal relating, with God and with one another. We must learn to both hear and speak in ways that form bridges between ourselves and the other.

The second struggle is to reintroduce love as a significant focus for clarity, especially as the intended fulfillment in all personal relationships. We can no longer merely complain that the word "love" has been diluted to a meaningless term. We need to learn how to live it. It is ironic, as Jean Luc Marion points out, that "philosophy" means the love of wisdom, but excludes discussion of the wisdom of love. Love is the great command in the Bible, but is not a major heading in theology books. Why is this? I assert that love is the North Star of our human quest to understanding personal relations. We must begin by setting our course with that magnetic attraction compelling us.

Chapter 2 introduces a key entry point into Christian thinking: the discovery that something is missing in how we engage relationship with our divine Father, and with humans as well. Jesus was a Father-centric person. He began each day focused on his Father, followed his Father's lead, and burst forward every day with love borne from the heart of his Abba Father. Our own human fathers, in their human imperfection, often confuse the idea of Father for us. We must come to a peace with our human fathers, but, more importantly, recognize that they are not in the same category as God the Father. But discussion of God the Father is missing from virtually all theology books. Ironically, to discover our deepest identity, we must rediscover the Abba of Jesus as our own Abba. We must be changed through discovering this One whom Jesus came to reveal to us (John 1:18). We find Jesus as a compass that points to a hidden but powerful home that calls us to shake the definitions that have shackled us to a warped vision of who we are. What is missing in our human understanding of love is filled, not with definitions, but with the One who promises to be our place of belonging. We cannot see this Father, but we can live each day within God's promise to surround us and guide us toward love fulfilled.

Chapter 3 opens up the possibility of discussion between God and humanity. If theological thinking is to go beyond mere theory, it must include dialog. Good theology cannot be merely about God, but must dialog with God in a personal manner. This is the point of Kevin Vanhoozer's work in rethinking the science of learning to understand God through the Bible: what scholars call "hermeneutics." In the Bible, the voice of God is the vehicle of personal encounter. The sheep are supposed to hear the Shepherd's voice. But this is a lost expectation for the modern mind. We usually expect silence. In this loss of connection that is our modern Enlightenment stance, having rejected God's voice for the voice of science, we are in need of revitalizing the missing voice that spans the space between us and creates personal relating. Walls must be removed, and bridges rebuilt.

Chapter 4 discusses what it means to be a person, and exposes the pseudo-selves we create that keep us from the relationships for which we were created. Even theologians who study what it means to be a person can miss how personhood plays out in our relationships. My story is one of awakening to this knowledge, realizing I had missed its practical application. But out of fractured experiences came an opportunity to be made anew. This process is not a mental assent to a set of beliefs; it is more like a storm that changes everything by taking us out of self-preoccupation. We are transformed into a gift-bearing extension of God's love. In daily trusting our bonded connection, we begin to breathe creativity in our lived space. If we do not understand what it means to be a person in a trusting relationship, we will forever dance with shadows. We will ache with the strain of almost hearing music too faint to get inside us and draw us into authentic, daily relating. But this is where good theology must lead us.

Chapter 5 engages the difficult topic of sin. Rather than being a law-based violation of abstract and alien principles, sin is unpacked as that which destroys relationships. Sin is not a thing that can be given its own status as an object having independent existence. Sin is the negative side of being connected in habits that ignore, violate, abuse, or injure others—a dynamic of mal-relating. In this same act against others, we warp our own character. So much theological thinking uses language that does not connect with our experience, or leaves us unconvinced there is really a problem. We feel the tension of knowing we are not perfect, but believe we should not be condemned for being human. Many people cannot see why Christianity focuses so dominantly on the sin problem. We must discover that an addictive nature plagues us all, as we medicate to deal with our pain and losses. Consequently, in order to move to an authentic existence, we must acknowledge our bentness and self-interest in order to move to healthy face-to-face relating.

Chapter 6 explores the concept of fear, which is the biblical opposite of love. N.T. Wright has stated that some form of the phrase "Do not be afraid" is the most common appeal in the New Testament. Fear is the core of our fractured existence. Theologically speaking, fear is what separates us from God's life, then spreads like cancer to our human relating. Fear is a neglected topic in theological discussion. I hope to bring a spotlight to accentuate the Bible's emphasized concern. Delving into fear's influence helps us see its full connection as an alienating stimulus. Fear is the central human emotion. In its many levels of intensity, it provokes self-centered distancing from God and neighbor, ranging from anxiety to terror. In this chapter, we get at the root of sin as what happens between us, not merely in us.

Chapter 7 finishes our inquiry into what is missing in our pursuit of personal, face-to-face relationships. We find that the habits in our interpersonal relating are intuitive expressions due to our conflicted relations with God and one another. I explore how addiction theory does not merely label a few warped individuals. It exposes the underlying forces of the fear-based life as the core operating system for humanity. Once we unveil this profound malfunction in our daily interactions, then we have hope to be reformatted in a manner spelled out in the central gospel themes of the Bible, namely the restoration of relationships toward healthy personal connection.

Sin is a concern for self. The word "synthetic" refers to human-made products. In this book, I contend that we have a "sin-thetic" life because, left to ourselves, we construct our own lives as individuals, overlooking consideration for God or neighbor. But a life apart from God is artificial. We are self-made. It feels good to be the master of our own life. Thus, I do not see sin as a life of being bad or breaking the rules. Rather, the sin-thetic life is a self-centered life that separates us from those we need (and who need us) to live a mutual life of love.

An authentic life is lived in a trusting openness with others, including God, in honesty and collaboration. I am all about a new vision that gets this kind of meaningful life, and does not default to legalistic religion or constraining morality. This book begins the process of transformation that opens up when we turn our hearts to meet God and others face-to-face.

Chapter 1

Reinhabiting the Garden of Love

"If you wish to be loved, love."

—*Seneca (Roman philosopher, mid-1st century AD)*

"When we lose one we love, our bitterest tears are called forth by the memory of hours when we loved not enough."

—*Maurice Maeterlinck (1862–1949)*

"God loved the birds and invented trees. Man loved the birds and invented cages."

—*Jacques Deval*

SOMETHING IS MISSING. NEVER before have we had such amazing tools and toys that allow us to flourish in our human experience; yet, at the same time, a gnawing hollowness spreads into the fibers of our personal relating. Relationships disintegrate, marriages become dissonant, families disengage, communities crumble, our nation divides, our global connections are tense, and God is a diminishing shadow in the public sphere.

The Garden of Eden experience of walking with God is a forgotten ideal in this reality-show-obsessed world. Yes, there are exceptions: the loving families and good neighbors who mirror God's original intention. But at the same time we are seeing huge advances, we are also experiencing profound breakdown. Scientists are mastering knowledge of the material world. Medicine is providing solutions to our fleshly frailty. Technology is developing an internetedness to our connectedness. But we are losing the threads of penetrating communication that weave together the many strata of our lives.

Where in this world can we find a serious investigation that engages the most important feature of human existence: our relationships? That is my quest, not for a misplaced Holy Grail, but for a "system restore" in the matrix of relating. We customarily bump each other's bubbles of "personal space," but yearn for an embrace that ignites the fire between us. We must rediscover who we are and how to meaningfully relate in simple strides that will build for a lifetime.

My initial step in this learning process was coincidental, but became a gift that formed my life's trajectory. My first grand move out of my childhood home was a gentle step to the house next door. In the tragic chess game of life, the neighbors had moved away, and thoughtless renters had scarred its beauteous face, leaving decades of tender gardening a paradise lost. However, I remembered what had been, and offered to invest my sweat as rent to recapture the cherished memory of the landscape I still held dear. Memory and dream moved my able hands.

I loved the verdant gardens and pleasance of the orchard, but there was a special place in my heart for the kitchen. I especially cherished its huge west-facing picture window, where an observer like me could survey the daily arrival of visitors, the palette of light as it swept through the day, and the ever-changing grounds bringing the joy—and demand for attention—of a two-year-old child in full sprout. Windows create anticipation. Kitchens complete the connection as a gathering place.

In that kitchen, I had many conversations with Bob, a friend who moved in to share what was beginning to feel like a restoration of the Sistine Chapel. One day he told me, "On my gravestone, I would like it to read, 'to have loved was enough.'" Though this sounded noble, something in me was unsettled, like trying to remember an old friend's name so you can look her in the eye and start a conversation. I could see the immediate appeal of living as a gift, and dying with the pleasure of knowing you were well spent. But there must be more. I was not yet satisfied.

I searched for what was missing like looking for the puzzle piece that brings a face into focus. Each addition brings a joy as it remembers home, a delightful resolve as fingers feel the homecoming. Then it came to me one day: I want to have been loved when I lay on my final resting bed (hoping not to experience one of those violent ends).

So the motto that came was, "To have loved and been loved, that was enough." Of course, at that time, just past the two-decades-old flag, I was hardly aware of how little I knew about what this might mean. It sounded beautiful and noble. I later came to see that the central task of theology as unfurled in the story of the Bible is to draw humans back into this life of loving and being loved, but not out of our human resources. We are called to live within the gift of love offered. That becomes the starting point for the logic of love that shapes a life of accepting and extending love in the economy of grace.

But we require new ears and eyes to overcome the controlling patterns of religious life. We must learn to see that, unfortunately, words can be tools of control that merely limit our world to another person's set of expectations. "I just want you to be happy" sounds so innocent and good-hearted, but often comes in the form of a cookie mold that squeezes us into someone else's happy end. For many, the Bible is construed as the Grand Editor of our lives. It has the feel of a tightly-corseted ideal to overcome the flabbiness of our humanity that misses God's supposed ideal. But the Bible is much more interested in relocating us into a life of love. It cannot take us on short vacations to "a place of happiness," especially when chosen by dysfunctional family or by traditions we do not own. The relationships that precede words are the heart's true location for finding the shared joy that fulfills our humanity. Words can bridge our lives, give us unsatisfactory imitations of connection, or become roadblocks to understanding.

Over the years, I have found that words do not have fixed meanings. They are more like recipes. In our use of them, we must learn both to be playful and to desire health.

Harvesting fresh garden produce, a family might create unique edible art. Each day's contribution creates a salad, but with lively, changing elements. It is still a salad, but new and nourishing even when components change. So with words, rather than fixed definitions, we need spirit-edly-grounded invitations to share meaning and to let our expressions keep growing and changing in conversation.

Everyone knows what coleslaw is, but have you tasted Grandma's? "Coleslaw" has many variations that are tied to the stories of each family; some taste amazingly the same (in institutions and stores), and some are wonderfully different with secret ingredients. Each word we speak has a recipe that is not the same for everyone. "Love" is not the same in every mind. For some it is distasteful; for others, it is a romantic delight.

We wish everyone thought like us in what they mean by each word. They do not. An entire sentence compounds the mystery, adding surprising meaning-ingredients to each salad. After some conversations and sermons we say, "Give me more of that!" Regrettably, some talks are either bitter or just don't agree with us. We do not like their recipe in how they use particular words. Words can seem plastic, as if their wrapping has spoiled the taste.

One of the great challenges of theological thinking is to get all the different denominations and traditions to retire their sense of authority to define God and their need to exclude those opinions that differ. Words become power trips, people fight over thoughts and beliefs, and love is lost. We need to let God be God, and to give up trying to tame God through artificial portraits that plaster our mental space. We need to be surprised by joy at how we are drawn into a life of continuity with the God who is daily guest at our table, and experience a full freshness in the conversation: always loving, but always in new ways.

"Love" is possibly the most varied word in the "recipes" that lie behind it. That has been confusing for me and maybe for you. Over the years, we learn to think out of our mother's use of love. We might easily assume our spouse means the same thing, and are later surprised to discover that only a few ingredients are the same. The differences can shock our palates and instigate debates about which is better. I have come to believe that we must accept each other's recipes without eating the ones that make us sick. We need to be willing to understand the differences, and keep learning how to improve our recipes. By this, I mean that we might hold our language lightly and openly, to recognize that just as every word has a recipe, so too, those we speak to each have their cherished approach. This is true in all theological endeavors as well; we need to learn to use language to connect and explore, not to win a war.

"To have loved" is not a formula to replicate. Rather, it is an invitation to initiate savored movements, sampling and sharing life with another unique person. Experiencing their careful recounting of stories of pain and loss, triumphs and passions, and patterns of touching becomes part of our own "recipe" for love. Loving creates the space for others to come out and play. Loving makes life monumental.

I had seen gravestones as a reminder of a life well spent but now ended. Thus, gravestones can be Death Markers, but for me, this recipe-phrase, "to have loved and been loved," became a Life Marker. It has given me an end-picture of what I want my daily involvements to look like so that the final reflection rings true and inspires the lives of others to take note and find their own story.

I had to learn these life skills the hard way. My life story is full of tending gardens and investing in meals to savor with others, but also wrestling through a divorce and remarriage. I spent two decades drinking deeply of higher education and learning from books, but have also collaboratively worked in five churches, each bringing a bounty of ingredients to my thinking, from the sweet to the substantially meaty. I have been a marriage and family therapist for over a decade, which has sculpted me during each session by exposing me to the complexities of human conflict, disappointment, and lost hope. But the light of hope is not lost to me. All these experiences have created a stained glass life of complexity through which my table is illuminated, spread with love-seasoned plates of edible art I invite others to share.

"To have loved and been loved" is a compass for me, giving a sense of location that helps to choose my direction.

The power of love influences me as if I am moved by a strong force, like the magnetic North Pole, which orients me to the direction I wish to explore. It also shows me how to find my way home.

Today, the meaning of this life-phrase is still a mystery to me. That being said, I could talk for hours about what it has meant. I am confident that in the future, new hints of flavor will season this motto. I imagine unleashed moments when this catch-phrase will burst into life. It is like sitting in a fine restaurant, trying to figure out what is contributing that delicious fragrance to the treasure steaming before me. I hope this book invites you to keep simmering and playing with the recipes that guide your journey.

I am convinced that the central task of theology today is to discover the God who embodies love. God speaks, and we may respond. All of our God-talk must find its original expression in God's game of love. If we say "God is love," we must see the specific actions that demonstrate love played out in human history. God is not as interested in abstract ideas of love as in inviting us to join in his ongoing story of love. We can still use language, metaphor, and visual images, but recognize they are mere reflections of God's dynamic reality, as recipe is to the filled plate before us. We must never be satisfied with the likeness and therefore miss the intimacy. We cannot systematize God like a pinned specimen to own and display. Rather, we must enter with mystery and wonder into God's relational system, a complex jungle bursting with divine life. God's life is not a museum to visit; it is an expansive garden of love from which to live.

You may wonder why I spend so much time talking of gardens, recipes, gravestones, and finding love. C.S. Lewis said—and I agree—that "Joy is the serious business of heaven." I further believe that love is the serious business of living on earth. But not just any kind of love will do. The dominant human urge is to satisfy ourselves and think we are being loved. For the quest on which we will embark, we must discover anew the gift of love from God, who is the source of self-giving love. This God lives the harmony of love, united in a dance of a reciprocal resonance between three persons. They live an extended embrace to one another that then shares in a dynamic life of gifting. This three-personed God is the fountain from which any truly other-centered human love arises. We need to taste their recipe of love, born on earth in a garden long ago, which overcomes all our inclinations to separation and selfishness. That feast of fulfillment is the hope for which I have written this book. I want you to live with anticipation beyond your failures and faltering, disappointment in others, struggle for fulfillment, as well as the joys and seasons of courage. I desire for you to be renewed into a life made possible by the Creator's love, that sings its deepest tune to invite you into a dance of delight. Divine love never lives in a soloed monotone. Creation and redemption are the initiation and final resolve in God's symphony, still playing over the centuries in expectancy of a grand resolution. God takes broken pasts and entwines them into a rugged wreath of beauty.

Time is not always kind to our cherished past; Westview Apartments now replace both my family home and my neighbor's property, my greenhouse of seminal thoughts and passions. The giant firs that still rim the edge of the combined properties are a living Stonehenge or ring of Ents standing in honor of the days that formed the culinary-gardener theologian I have become.

Although that past is gone, what remains is a deep ache in my soul for intimate relating that goes back to my childhood. For most of us, that yearning is the sign of what is still missing. You may be numb to it. Or you may feel that longing is the surest sign you are alive. But for me, the ache only became obvious during the storms of my life, when the rain fell and dormant seeds of unrecognized needs began to sprout.

Chapter 2

Discovering Father

"The greatest man I never knew lived just down the hall,
And every day we said hello but never touched at all."

—*Reba McEntire*

"Fear is static that prevents me from hearing myself."

—*Samuel Butler*

"Parents are often so busy with the physical rearing of children
that they miss the glory of parenthood, just as the grandeur of
the trees is lost when raking leaves."

—*Marcelene Cox*

IF JESUS HAD WRITTEN a theology book, chapter one would
have been about his Father. Yet this chapter is missing
from almost every theology book written. Where so many
have a difficult relationship with their human fathers, Jesus
deeply loves his Father. This beloved Son desires that we
interpret all his words and actions as an overflowing of his
Father's love, moving every act of his earthly life. Jesus is

never an end in himself. He is on a mission to bring us home to his Father who is to be our Father. People who love Jesus but forget his Father have lost who Jesus really is. The Spirit is on a similar venture, whose greatest act is to enable us to cry out "Abba, Father," meaning we have found our way back to the Family of the Father as his child.

But if we are to have a relationship with Jesus as *he* wishes it, we need to address our Father-voids, those "missing-persons" scars that bring up questions like, "Where were you?" or, "Why couldn't you love me?" The challenge to be made whole is deepened because our human and divine fathers are not the same, though they may both feel distant. The loss makes us afraid and alone, diminishing our view of who we are.

But we must be clear that God the Father is not just a big blow-up of human fatherhood. Our human fathers do not reveal Jesus's Father. God the Father is a class of his own. Only Jesus can show us his Father. That is the starting point for theology, the study of God. We might all have immediate access to our human fathers who can either make us feel huggable and cherished, or they may lay foundations of self-neglect and unworthiness. Unconditional love is not basic to their human nature. They, too, had inadequate fathers. Even the absent ones are tragically present by their nonappearance.

We need to make peace in the human sphere of relating, but even more with God the Father in the divine sphere. God only loves us; love is God's basic nature. But so many images and stories devastate our picture of who he is and how he feels about us. With our human fathers, we must learn to accept their imperfection and inadequacy. We must stop resisting them, and release them so they do not keep us anchored in the emotional battles that control us, sometimes over the way they acted, and sometimes over their neglect.

What is missing in life often creates strong currents that carry us for years. This is the story of my relationship with my dad. Growing up, I profoundly respected my dad's intelligence. His love and talent for teaching and learning "outside the box" drew me with confidence into a shared world of education. His pursuit of higher education to the Master's level made it emotionally plausible to go further myself, which I did for an extra-long academic jog of twenty years. Amazingly, I do not remember anyone ever encouraging me to go to college. However, I became a teacher in my dad's nonconformist footsteps, though in a very different field. We both loved to see others learn. But I did not know if my father loved me.

If I wanted others to learn, I had to become a learner. My dad wanted people to learn science, to be able to interpret the physical world. I wanted people to learn about relationships that were deeper than those I had seen modeled at home or at church. This development came in phases. Through my involvement with Young Life,[1] I learned about the necessity of relationships in a meaningful life. Through Bruce Larson's[2] work, I first felt the call to Relational Theology as a practical discipline I could get excited about. But sadly, I saw relational thinking rejected in the academy of theological thought. This created a fire in me to discover or develop an intellectually acceptable defense for this relational vision, one that was theologically grounded but spoke into the wonderful world of human connecting. Bruce had a heart for everyday persons and thus dismissed

1. Young Life is a youth outreach program based on building relationships on school campuses.

2. Bruce Larson was a Presbyterian minister who wrote books on the Christian life being all about relationships.

the Academy's criteria for style, method, and agenda. He tried to keep it simple and personal. But I was convinced that he had a key to unlock the practical implications of the Bible.

Later, I desired to give an intellectual response to my father's loss of faith in Christianity. Though the son of a Presbyterian minister, my dad was disillusioned during a conversation about prayer when a minister commented, "sometimes we have to fake it for a good cause." "But," my dad thought, "if we fake it sometimes, how do we know when the faking stops?" This avalanched his faith and impacted his assessment of Christianity's entire belief system. As a science teacher converted out of Christianity, his empirical method became his faith system. The simpler arguments of science expelled the need for a complex, non-material God he could not physically grasp.

I never felt oppressed by my dad; I was merely a resident in lengthening shadows of being unknown. My memories are mostly of silent years. Whether we stayed at home, or drove around the country in shared pursuits of car parts for old Chevys, redeeming these neglected and rejected relics was our "family religion." I still remember an outing, somewhere between Seattle and Reno, where my dad asked about my thoughts on the presidential race. This shocked me, as this was the first time in my life that my opinion was invited to step into the light of day. So much of my opinion was held inside for fear of being either discounted or misunderstood. What mostly stopped me was the dread of not being heard.

As I recall, the first time my dad ever hugged me was when, at thirty-two years old, I was departing for New Zealand for several years. Although my dad was not very affectionate or emotionally available, I desperately wanted his respect. That might have come from joining his conversations with uncles and brothers, from which I felt excluded. I was a person of faith, and believed I could not swim in their intellectual waters. What I wanted was an affection that may best be expressed with attention.

My life finally changed. Through my own process of discovering my inadequacies, I began to recognize that if I wanted a different relationship with my dad, I would need to be the active agent of change. Along with the rest of my family, I had lived for years with a shouting silence regarding an indiscretion of my dad's. I responded to my counselor one day, as to why I did not initiate challenging conversations with my dad, saying "Because I love him and do not want to hurt him." He calmly responded, "I think you have confused love and fear. It feels like love to you, but all I hear is your fear of having a real relationship." His insight was a flood of fresh spring air.

So I went to my dad and said, "I have a story in my head that you do not love me, and there are things about you I do not understand, but want to know. Would you be willing to tell me?" He was amazingly open, and we surfed the waves of past events for about three hours. Together we left nothing in veiled silence. He told me he had wished to talk about these things, but never could. What outside viewers could only see as an affair had also been a long-term friendship with an incredible woman, a memory for which he felt neither pride nor regret. His ongoing love for my mom was evident. He was at peace with his life; our talk brought serenity to me as well.

Additionally, my dad gave me examples of what he had intended to be acts of love, though I had never heard their loving intent. These included building me a small wheelbarrow and taking me to swap meets, where herds of car enthusiasts searched for the puzzle pieces to transform their old cars into prized possessions, instead of the pile of metal in the garage that the wife wished would go away. As we conversed, my life was finding its own lost pieces.

We cannot change the past, but we can get over judging it. Forgiveness now frames his life in a gentler way as a person living his own story. To stop resisting our fathers ends our own self-sculpting of our emotional life as we shove against them. Even when dads die, they don't vacate our emotional space; we still have thick callouses from our persistent resistance against their influence. Acceptance allows us to see who we might be when shaped by love.

During this time in my life, I came to believe that love must overcome the fears that imprison us. I lived a kind of delusion through detachment. I defaulted to living on the sidelines of my father's life: observing, but not getting on the field of real relating. I was not looking for a perfect new relationship with my dad, just an honest one that would allow an authentic connection to grow, accepting our differences. We walk in that direction now.

This whole experience has been a deep upgrade in daily life: to live in love, and let go of fear, which is the opposite of love. Perfect fear makes one concerned about self, and forgets the consequences for others. When I am afraid in public conversations, I hide to protect myself. Mature love allows me to respect myself, and to move with a concern for others, without fear of loss. Perfect fear casts out love. Perfect love casts out fear.

To love and be loved requires me to honestly recognize that fear makes me a people pleaser afraid of rejection. Fear brings out a perfectionist performing to earn love that is conditional. Masks then cover emotions to conceal those authentic feelings and desires of which others might disapprove. Love, however, can stealthily break the logjams of stuck feelings.

Theology must include a practical language that gets at the core of how we relate with our family of origin. It must help us understand the emotional level of the human experience. We can no longer pretend that good teaching "in the head" is sufficient to bring "salvation"; only *God's* healing of our fear, pain, and stuckness can restore us. We need to see God bring wholeness to our challenged familial contexts. We cannot just have Bible studies about what the prophets and apostles meant; we must see what they mean today in our lived space.

The other significant breakthrough in my life opened my vision to what I might know about God, specifically the Father. Like my own dad, who could fix anything, but was distant, so God also seemed capable and dependable, but too busy to be there to express care for me. One night I heard Brennan Manning[3] speak. I sat mesmerized as he unpacked the grace of God. God spoke of the patient heart of the Father. Jesus came to reveal his Abba as One who embraces us with a delighted, crazy-love. God will never let us go, or allow us to condemn ourselves for "not being good enough." Never before had I seen the amazing, unfathomable richness that exists between Father and Son. But Brennan's voice and honest stories of his own failure and God's acceptance penetrated to the deep recesses of my soul, especially as he taught us to pray, "Abba, I belong to you." In that room, I saw a man who had been broken and ashamed, but then lifted to the tenderest embrace by Almighty God. As the tears dried and I could read the Bible with new eyes to see this passionate Father, I wished to never leave that mystery who was revealed as True North. Prayer now meant to enter that embrace and know my

3. Brennan Manning was an author and speaker who was a Catholic priest before he married. His books convey a profound experience of grace.

heart's true home. Too often I had experienced prayer as a life of wishful begging. But that night, I found a place of acceptance instead of neediness.

I left that experience stunned. I walked into my friend's house as in a daze. When asked if I was OK, these words came out of my mouth, "I feel like an egg that has just been peeled. All my life to this point, a crust has separated me from God. But tonight the shell is peeled back and I feel soft and supple." It felt like being born anew into a bigger family. Prayer went from begging to belonging.

The most penetrating thought introduced by Brennan that night was, "If you took all the love of all the fathers and mothers that ever lived and put them together, that would be but a single drop in the ocean of love that the Abba of Jesus has for us." I cannot imagine anyone measuring the gallons in the seas, much less drops in the ocean. This thought immediately flooded me with a sense of bathing in an overwhelmingly deep and profoundly mysterious love.

This immersion in God's love has got to be the entrance point of an adequate theology. If we miss a deep soaking in the love of the One Jesus came to not only reveal, but to radically reunite us with, we will forever whisper of love, but never taste its sweetness.

This transforming occasion was part of the divine healing that took me beyond my dad's inadequacies. That night, I was finally aware of Abba's embrace. I still struggled to let go of my complaints and accept my earthly father, but I learned that I do not need to prove anything to anyone, especially my father. I needed to let love in, and allow my images of God to be healed by the overwhelming love of my discovered Abba. This baptism in being loved sustains me to this day and helps me experience a new manner of Christian familial existence. I belong loved. Any adequate theology must establish this life of love as the core criteria in being able to hear what God makes known in the Bible.

If we do not see the life, death, and resurrection of Jesus as a clear vision that we are loved by our Abba, then we will hang precariously on the scaffolding of trying to get to God. We will be distracted from the divine grace that surrounds us. Once we discover what it means to be held, we will become articulate at describing the Father's work in our particular story. Theology then moves from abstract argumentation to the daily dance of partners.

Love is more than a concept or a feeling; that old idea must die. We need to leave the comfort of isolation, of thinking the life of love is "out there" or "in me." We must be reborn in loving dialog. We must discover this amazing thing called a relationship that is like a plant that grows between us. When we talk, it is watered. When we fume and cogitate alone in silence, the plant dies.

Dialog is not just that I talk to you and you volley back. It is the creation of a third thing that is the life between us. We cannot see it, but we can discern when it is there and when it is missing. Life feels hollow. When you discover the Abba of Jesus, you discover the source of authentic love for that life. When you discover Jesus's voice, you find the One who lives the dialog from the Father directed to you. He is sent to facilitate your knowing the Father, and to awaken you to know you are passionately known. When you discover the Spirit, you are given ears to hear the heart of the Father. Through the voice of the Son, you are addressed as a child who comes to know that you have a relationship that is a gift from God, but it needs watering. You may just see empty space with your eyes. But it is meaning-filled space when you come to know that another person has reached out to meet you through that space. Connection is made when you reach back. That vision does not make the learning of love easy or a joy-filled progression. My experience of this process was like the prolonged pain of childbirth. But we are promised new life is there for those who cross the threshold. Relational health is never just about me; it is about we.

Chapter 3

Voices in the Stark Night

"Love is seeing without eyes, hearing without ears; hatred is nothing."

—*Doug Horton*

"Become a student of change. It is the only thing that will remain constant."

—*Anthony J. D'Angelo*

"If a man does not keep pace with his companions, perhaps it is because he hears a different drummer. Let him step to the music which he hears, however measured or far away."

—*Henry David Thoreau*

ASKING THE RIGHT QUESTIONS is usually more important than finding the right answers. Questions open the field for exploration; answers fool you into thinking you have arrived. This is especially true when learning about God. The silence is deep and the night is stark when there is a void in hearing and being heard. The landscape is littered with memorials to those who sculpted definitive statements on what God is like and how we must live. But the Spirit blows like a searching wind, and erodes those stones one breath at a time. Then amidst the rubble, in times of change, God speaks again.

In the academic world, it is said that theology is "talk about God," but that statement unintentionally leaves God as a silent, sitting-in-the-corner object outside our conversation. This is too much like the grandparents who sit and hear their adult children talk about their future as though they are not there. Often we feel left out when it comes to being understood, including by the people we regularly sit with. I suggest that the most helpful task of theology is to learn to hear what God has been saying and is speaking about. Then we may respond to the invitation to live in an ongoing interchange called a personal relationship. While we may experience times when we wish the other could "really hear" us, so does God. Worthy theology is about a conversational relationship that achieves mutual understanding between us and our divine partner. Good theology helps us break free of the separating walls that seem so normal, in order to facilitate dialog. But we must start in the appropriate place.

In seeking to know God or another person, some start from revelation, and some from reason. This is a critical distinction, but what does that mean? Nutshell—one approach listens to learn; the other interprets how another fits within the categories of our experience. This distinction is simple, but enormous in implications.

Revelation is about hearing the voice of another person. But not just the audible voice. We must learn to deeply listen to the core commitments of the other person. Paying careful attention to the unfolding drama of their backstory, we become students of the unique way this person has been shaped to communicate, and we find what motivates them. When we reflect, "It sounds like you are really committed to X," they might respond, "Yes! I finally feel like I am being heard; I just could not find the words." This is deep listening. We cannot merely listen to words or emotions; we must learn to hear heart commitments.

Like adjusting binoculars to get the clearest image possible, one learns to "bring into focus" another person's manner of communicating. In the same way, we may hear a speech by Martin Luther King, Jr. We know his intonation and articulation. But his "voice" speaks out in so many other ways in events, speeches, celebrations, and reverberations. These all find their clear source in him, and carry his "voice" to new situations and generations. Voice speaks from the heart and history of a person.

When I assert that good theology is based in revelation, it is like the opening of a rose to show itself in its own way and its own time. I am seeking to help you find fresh ways to hear God speaking in continuity with what is revealed in Jesus. In a sense, we have a choice at a fork in the road. We either give our opinion about what God thinks (being reasonable), or we find a rapt way of listening to him (revelation). I am committed to creative clarity in attending to God's voice, and to allow my speaking to reverberate from his. Does Martin Luther King speak today? Like never before. Does God speak today? Profoundly, but we must learn how to hear God's voice.

Reason, on the other hand, employs human experience. One reflects on their life experience, and that becomes the focus of study. "That's reasonable to me" means your claim fits in with my individual experience. But my experience may be different from yours. You may think I am unreasonable because we interpret differently. In the rational mode of discovery, the human ultimately becomes the arbiter as to what to believe or reject. We become judges with self-protective interests. We resist looking unreasonable or getting hurt. The internal evaluator of what is reasonable will not believe many claims of truthfulness; we have a basic mistrust of what we do not know. Some people exclude all ideas that are inconsistent with collections of "facts" that form scientific truthfulness; they have a bias to believe only the humanly provable. But science only studies the world of objects. This makes understanding persons unreasonable to the one who believes we are only objects. The reasonable mind resists all things "emotional" or "subjective" as biased or mere opinion. This also excludes the arts, the humanities, religion, and everyday relationships as the focus of serious study. But we need a science of persons that explores the complexities of our nature.

In the "reasonable" paradigm, sameness is valued and uniqueness is questioned. We can only study persons as they fit into categories of sameness (gender, age, race, etc.). Thus, unique voices are excluded, favoring instead the common voice of "what every reasonable person believes." This myth would like us to think "everyone agrees with me." It neglects paying attention to the distinctiveness of each voice. So if you say to someone, "Tell me who you are," they will answer you by giving a reasonable explanation for why they exist, what they do, and what they are about. But in the end, you will only know the carefully chosen pieces that fit their cookie cutter persona; their distinctives remain hidden.

The primary task of theology is to hear what the voice of God is saying to God's people today, not merely what was said long ago. This present listening is facilitated by the Holy Spirit, who gives us ears and eyes to interpret Jesus's speaking to us. I am not advocating a wild mysticism that just "listens" to your experience of sunset and peaceful moments to hear God. That would be no different from a reasonable scientist who only listened to their own experience and not to other people; they would be isolated in their own head. But through the Spirit, over time, we come to personally know the author and voice of the Bible. We hear the heart of Jesus's Father, from which he speaks and acts personally for those to whom the Father extends an embrace. This is a different kind of reasoning that flows from the revelation of God's love. As the great philosopher Pascal said, "Love has reasons that reason does not know." The life of relationships is not unreasonable; it merely values persons over objects in its practice. Conversely, scientists cannot be impersonal in any part of life; they will always act as persons in their investigations and interactions. As Michael Polanyi[1] said, "All knowledge is personal knowledge," because all the findings of science are made by persons called scientists, interpreted by other persons, and developed by other persons. Knowledge is personal. Knowledge of persons is a more complex personal knowledge.

The fulfillment of our personal lives can seem like such a solitary, self-created task. We are happy with relationships when they fit into our schedule, as long as they do not interrupt too much. But the current of daily tasks sweeps us along. Eventually, movement becomes mistaken for meaning. We are controlled by the pressure of "doing enough" each day to feel we have justified our existence. But we miss that relationships are core to who we are, and that we must understand them in order to be fulfilled.

Relationships are fragile and easily damaged. Some affiliations never fully materialize from their embryonic state. Some friendships rise above the mundane and give us sanity. Good or bad, they all sculpt our emotional world.

1. Michael Polanyi was a philosopher of science who called into question its claim to objectivity.

I do not know if meltdowns in life are necessary to awaken hidden insights that need releasing, but I have had my share. And God has used challenges to help me hear his voice.

In my early twenties, I was still quite shy. Confidence was an acquired taste unnatural to me. I had just enough courage to ask, as a friend, questions like, "How can I help you, encourage you, or make a way for your gifts to be used?" But occasionally I was a blind fool, oblivious to the dangers of trying to console and counsel the wrong people.

The coming disruption sent no warning. In my youthful innocence, I found the ground torn from beneath me in a cold reality. I learned that even good people go through messy misunderstandings, and the shrapnel cuts deep.

This occurred three decades ago. As a single youth pastor, the lead pastor's wife developed a deep affection toward me. I was twenty-four, and she thirty-eight, and I had no idea that any woman that much older would be attracted to someone my age. She was not entirely happy in her marriage, and I was an attentive listener. Nothing more than a hug ever happened. I stopped meeting with her when I recognized she was becoming emotionally attached. Months later, I was called into the pastor's office and informed that her counselor had urged her to "confess" her story. My great error was that I had met with her as a friend alone. As one might imagine, this caused a wave of reactive fear in her husband. I was relieved of my responsibilities both at the church and as a Young Life leader. Fortunately, the couple stayed married and engaged in marital surgery. I wrestled alone.

Even now, it is hard to tell my story without fearing that blame will be unnecessarily flung, assigned to now-wiser hearts. It is difficult to discern who really crossed what lines, but the hatchet's fall was sure. In their pain, my accusers could not hear my innocent intentions. I felt a great plunge, experienced in that moment when you drop into water and all sound ceases in the alien world of isolation.

The outcome of the fiasco was expulsion from ministry, which was my life. Questions seized my brain: How could this happen to me? All I could hear were unresolved internal voices of deliberation. I felt amputated.

A quiet breath of grace came one day as I sat on a bench by a meandering river that seemed to be going nowhere fast. Like Elijah the prophet, I was crushed by aloneness and abandonment. I could not hear God in the events that swept me along. In this turmoil of desperation, I heard a Voice internally whispering, "I love you."

I had never been addressed by an audible voice I thought was God's. I still have not. This loving, internal voice could be taken as just another instance of my internal dialog, the voice in my head that asks, "What voice in my head?" Gently, this soft voice came rolling into my awareness.

I was perched on the edge between accepting mystery or retreating to a dismissive certainty that no one was there. If there is one phrase I could possibly acknowledge as an authentic whisper from God, it would be this affirming phrase of love. I was faced with a choice: to continue to believe that life with God is silent (or that I do all the talking) . . . *or* accept this possibility that God invites me to start with the simple act of believing this affirming phrase as an address from a real person. The deepest source of God's voice comes from the Father's heart, is enacted in the life of the Son, and is offered by the Holy Spirit. God's three-fold voiced affirmation of love is arguably the main message of the Bible. The question is always whether or not I will listen.

In that moment by the river, I was birthed into what has become a practice of my life: embracing personal relationships by accepting the other's voice as authentic. I realized that a "personal relationship" must flow between hearts through the gift of words that both parties mutually accept and own.

In that stark night, I learned to hear.

I am a self-starter, so it had always been easy for me to perform for God: to be a good person; to be a self-motivated, disciplined athlete; to get high marks in school. But over the years, I had inadvertently erected a wall between God and me as performance replaced closeness. I had operated out of managed appearances to look spiritual. Hesitantly, I hoped the dawning dialog of love would be like a crack in my own Berlin Wall as it began to crumble. Entering this unwrapped place and awakening to the voice's embrace has made sense of my world ever since. Honestly, that insight did not come all at once; it has been patiently wind-sculpted over time.

The enormity of hearing God's voice lay in glimpsing a landscape in which I might flourish. It reminds me of the first time I stood before the fields of lupines that covered the hills in New Zealand. Gorgeous acres were started there with a packet of seeds, eventually transforming the landscape with seemingly unending beauty. Not everyone likes lupines, especially those persons whose fields are overrun by their invasiveness. Not everyone understands my being addressed by God, but for me, both are experiences of the awesome "otherliness" of God's beauty. Accepting God's living voice provided a fertile field for the sprouting of encounter. Was I worried about self-deception? Sure, but I was more worried that I might lose the reality of real relating, and never learn to trust God as bigger than my fear.

In time, I learned to hear the Bible as the voice of God. Not just to listen for "the Man upstairs," but to hear phrases mediate the particular voices of Father, Son, and

Spirit in the same way you hear the voice of a loved one in their written correspondence. This way of listening to God has shaped my whole journey: conceiving the work of theology (God-talk) as being in conversation with the three-personed God. I am not a theologian who tries to prove God's existence with unshakable certainties. I listen to the Bible, believing God wants to be known. And I think God firstly reveals God—God's life of self-giving love and intimacy—before speaking to what I think I need to know. God's expressed love precedes my whining or wishing. This is the logic of God's self-giving love: God has given God's self, and continues to give, whether or not we do anything. That is unconditional love that speaks and acts. Any other theological approach talks over God, and hears little or nothing.

Any voice brings me into an engagement with another. Each person speaks to their situations in ways appropriate to their audience, whether near or far, young or old, wise or simple. Yet all the expressions speak in a manner consistent with the central commitments of the persons themselves. This is how I hear God through the Bible's authors. Their rich diversity is an outworking of the voice of God to different occasions and peoples, yet the same personal God speaks.

That God would speak to me, saying, "I love you," moved me beyond making God's love merely an abstract theological point. God could see me sitting on a bench, alone and in anguish, and could awaken me out of my misery. God could plunge me into a different world—not to isolation, but to inclusion—into anticipating, awakening to hear the voice of God that heals by presence and attention.

I was learning to be a relational theologian, and just beginning to distinguish my work from systematic theology. By that I mean that rather than attempting to arrange the teachings of the Bible into sections that describe God and God's work in an orderly manner, I was learning to hear God's voice in the Bible to cultivate how relationships work through dialog. It requires listening and learning to converse in response.

Imagine that we are at a symphony. The symphony's composer is present, not as a spectator, but as an involved performer. The conductor who stands in front of the orchestra in this scenario has a double attention, both paying attention to the composer-performer, as well as guiding the orchestra. This conductor, like a theologian, lives in the unique place of "standing between" as a participant, not an outside observer. In this case, the conductor, when in concert, both follows and leads, bringing chosen elements to the fore, based on his/her personal interpretation, but interactively with the composer-performer. Relational theology is like the playing of a music score; it is both responsive and creative. It is a baptism into God's gift of engaging all persons who enter into the family community to play their unique part. However, we need not listen as a passive audience, but as the orchestra, ready to play and listen as the conductor-theologian leads us in playing out the composer's intent.

The Bible is a score to inspire improvisation, not a recording to provide background ambiance.

How we listen to the Bible depends on how we choose our points of view: We can either be an observer (audience) or a participant (artist). When we study the Bible, should we determine a set of right beliefs, or should we focus on hearing Jesus and entering the dialog? Many pursue the first, but never engage the second. I want both. This is like asking whether you want people to meet you first or to read your resume to get to know you. We want personal relations, but we settle for caricatures instead of encounters.

We frequently read the Bible as a memorial about an absent God. But we might aspire to meetings where we hear the voice of God call us home, and live there every day.

Hear me, please; I would not dispense with the Bible any more than I would dismiss the value of the cards and letters I get from my wife. But I want my focus of listening to be oriented to the persons (divine and human) who stand behind the writings, and to hear their voices addressing me in a dialog that brings that relationship to life. Thus, I call myself a relational theologian: one who listens and lives within dynamic relationships, not just one who talks about them. All meaningful theology is for the sake of living relationships.

My experience of loving and being loved grows as I learn how to stay within these theological conversations. Listening to God's voice is not merely a choice. It is a way of loving, a way of being with God or another person, knowing that I am known specifically, accepted with my inadequacies, and invited to grow with the other person by bringing my thoughts and feelings to the table. Someone holds me dear and discusses life with me.

I can never hear the word "revelation" again as a great download from the sky of "truths" from or about God. Revelation is like that blossoming rose that captures our attention, opening us up to experience the fullness of beauty and to be changed in the inhaling.

Years later, a letter came with an apology from those who wielded what I now see as a scalpel. Generosity of spirit has healed the wounds; understanding that ignorance is present in each of us has silenced all blame. Like the end of an Ice Age, I have emerged from the frozenness of stifled silence, and heard the Beloved call. I still respond to those soft, tender, beckoning words in the stark night of my soul.

God's revelation has whispered into my story, inviting me into God's story, and I am a humbled listener.

Profound loss and renewal marked that season of my life as I was being prepared to hear God. But my soul was to undergo deeper and more centered surgeries in learning to be a whole person. Further scarring would mark my life in a fierce, refining storm that blindsided me, but opened my eyes to see who I really am and what it means to trust in another person to take the next step forward.

Chapter 4

The Unforeseen Storm

"No man is an island, entire of itself; every man is a piece of
the continent, a part of the main. If a clod be washed away
by the sea, Europe is the less, as well as if a promontory were,
as well as if a manor of thy friend's or of thine own were: any
man's death diminishes me, because I am involved in mankind,
and therefore never send to know for whom the bell tolls; it
tolls for thee."

—*John Donne*

"Divorce is the psychological equivalent of a triple coronary
bypass. After such a monumental assault on the heart, it takes
years to amend all the habits and attitudes that led up to it."

—*Mary Kay Blakely*

"Birds sing after a storm; why shouldn't people feel as free to
delight in whatever remains to them?"

—*Rose Kennedy*

THE GREAT QUESTION OF our era is, "What does it mean to be a person?" Why is this so? Because we believe that we are individuals who live as bubbles that merely bump up against one another. We have thought we are isolated brains with bodies that chauffeur our thinking selves around. We have missed the idea that developing our interactive emotions and relations is the primary task of "personal growth." We have learned to wear masks for every occasion, and have lost the skill of being authentic selves without fear. This leaves our internal worlds ready for a perfect storm of anxiety and depression.

We consider anthropology to be the study of humans as physical, cultural, social, philosophical beings, and that is partly right. We do have bodies, develop in cultures, interact socially, and think about life. But we are also spiritual, relational, unique, and created to be in friendships with a fresh flow of knowing and being known every day.

Traditional anthropology looks for what is the same in all of us. It explores how we believe, celebrate, develop physically and culturally, and fit people into descriptive categories. Beneficial theological anthropology notices what is unique in all of us, but as part of a network of relations. Our distinctiveness is the result of the particular set of persons with whom we live in dialog. This includes the specific qualities of each relation. Who we "are" is always "going out of ourselves" to touch and feel the tingle of interaction with another. We send focused words, or bathe in a captured glance. We retort with cutting remarks. We develop familiar tones, and cultivate well-rehearsed routines. At the same time, we are "receptors of others," those persons who are going out of themselves to interlace with us in a similar manner, but with their own distinctive style. We exist as persons in this web of relatedness.

Sure, you have a body of blood and bones, but you are more. Of course, that body grows and spurts, limits us and gives us possibilities, but you exceed that. You are personal because you were not made as a rock in a field (just material) or left in the wild to grow (just biological). You were nurtured into being a person in the field of personal relations. That field is a complex network of family and friends, but also includes all the others you interact with along the way.

We are generally blind to this matrix of relations. If every person we met with left some visual trace of the relation, like planes leave a trail in the sky, we would see an immense grid of linked lines that form our field. But looking only through our eyes limits our thinking to a narrow scope where we think we stand at the helm of our head and look out at the world as mere space within which everything moves. Each of us thinks, "I am a self-sufficient, self-determining intelligence (who happens to have a body), and that is the world out there. We are separate." That may describe the experience of being a human. But to be a person is to go beyond the self-reflective, physical life. When you engage the heart and mind of another who reflects back to you, and then you reflect back to them, you are partaking in the life of persons in relation. To not be in relation is to not be personal. Loss of relations carves our personhood as well, reforming who we are as we move into who we are becoming.

And how blind to the future we can be! I married at age twenty-seven, thinking I was appropriately mature. Thirteen years later, without warning, a storm hit. I did not see it coming. Woefully clueless to an approaching marital breakdown, I thought I was in the golden years of my life. But I stumbled into a cyclone, learning the lessons of loving by seeing what I had missed.

Divorce is never a solitary act, but this is my story, not hers, so I will try to stay focused on what I learned.

I had believed myself to be an exemplary husband, and many friends agreed with me. I failed to realize I lacked the skills necessary to hear my wife's needs and meet her specific desires. I was a great husband by the books, but I now realize that love requires a specific knowing: accepting and responding to the one with whom you are actually building a marriage. Whatever may be true for most spouses does not necessarily have any actual bearing on the unique one standing in front of you. I was an expert at planning themed, romantic dates (e.g., Mango Tango improvised through poetry, lotions, and more). Nevertheless, to this day, I do not really know what she actually wanted. I do know she did not want me as I was. I was not fully a person as I tried to play a role. A role is a replacement for a relationship, a replica and not the real thing.

Additionally, I could not really be myself. Trying to be a "good boy" through my life had locked me in a prison of stuffed emotions. I was shocked to discover my comfortable persona had masked my face without invitation; my real self became a stranger trapped within. Sitting in a marriage counselor's office one day, having just shown him my poem, "The Cry of the Screaming Soul," our wise facilitator astutely observed that my outward appearance was that of a Golden Retriever, with happy, eager anticipation beaming from my face. But in my poem, I revealed a very different person inside, screaming out to be noticed, loved, affirmed, and valued. I was blind to my own disconnectedness. I was a divided self. I was incongruent. I did not really know what I felt; thus, I could not express my emotions. Congruent persons can name what they feel, and have the courage to say it. They live a transparency that is authentic. They are emotionally available to the other to live suitably connected.

But I could not see the fracturedness of myself. Thinking myself strong, I could not see my anemic relationship ability. Often, a strong individual makes a weak relationship. This is because strong personalities focus on themselves, and do not feed the "plant" that is the relationship between. A relationship is like a plant that needs attention, feeding, and pruning. Two less self-assured persons are more likely to invite the other to feed the "plant." They have the humility to recognize they are incomplete without the input of the other. Each is open to work through issues, asking, "I need help; will you help me think this through?" As a result, each shared agreement between the two creates a stronger relationship. They are in a growth process discovering who they are in a trusting relationship with the other.

I was so successful at impression management that I had lost connection with the paneled den of my emotional world. Inside was a neglected place where my dormant dreams and desires slumbered. On calmer days, I had meandered into believing that looking good was the road to being loved and affirmed. I had become a facade of loving; but hidden inside, a deeper well of artesian spring water bubbled. Storms can be ruinous to our safe trodden ways, and they can expose secreted places in need of fresh air.

I still remember the surrealism of driving away the day my former wife asked me to leave. I connected with none of her reasons. She had just returned from an initial visit with her first-ever individual counselor. For many months, I believed this was just a passing mistake. Gradually, I came to see that I had been replaced. I, the Golden Retriever, did not know her or myself. Friends and family shared stories that helped me glimpse her unhappiness; when considered together, the effect on me was like jerking back a veiling sheet. I saw I had been relationally blind. In New Zealand, I had seen a comedy act which portrayed a husband in the kitchen with "domestic blindness," unable to see what was right in front of him in refrigerator, closet, and pantry. I saw a new application of this truth in my personal relating. My journey since then has not been so much to figure her out, but to understand my own weaknesses, and to practice what I preach. This has been humbling and exciting. I feel like someone who has discovered the cure for a disease no one knows they have, but it is rampant everywhere.

After my divorce, I learned I had been out of control by trying so hard to be in control. I had carefully arranged my life to make sure no one, especially my former wife, would be upset. I gave other people's emotional responses priority over mine. Yes, I discovered I am a people pleaser. People pleasers lose themselves to become masks that please another. One counselor told me that to avoid upsetting other people is like handing them the steering wheel of my life. I go where they want, fearing their response if I don't. Their emotional world trumps mine. This is a tragic, but real relation as a shadow looking for affirmation. I needed to recover a sense of self-love: that dignity we grant ourselves to affirm our choices without being inconsiderate to others.

Personally, I do not like the word "self"; it feels so inward-focused. I prefer the word "person," as in "personal" relationship. This identifies my sense of being distinctively shaped in the warp and woof of relationships into which I have been woven. The term "self" is like "apartment" for me, a living very close to people, but being alone or separated-apart. I did not want to continue a self-alone existence. I already knew this in theory; my PhD was on the nature of being a person. Now I had to learn to be a person in my own skin.

This included investing as dad in my kids during the small islands of time they were with me, and learning to accept I was still their dad when they were away. My personhood was not shaped only when I was with them, but by a continuing attitude of connection when gone. Anger at the fact that I was largely edited out of my children's lives eventually melted into acceptance and enjoyment of the time we had. But flashes of emotional lightning were delivered in the process. The storm surged for months, and left damage for years.

Next, I learned that the flip side of "being out of control" is "needing to be right," spawned from the fear of being wrong. We all want to be right and good, but this is dangerous. Needing to be right, or rightness, makes others wrong. Rightness threatens relationships by producing either confrontations or seclusion. When others need to be right, we experience it as being controlled. Rightness splinters relationships. I needed to identify and shed old patterns that eroded my personal connections. New tools were vital for a calm after the storm.

The subtle use of the word "should" in my daily conversation was an old emotional crowbar that I used whenever I needed to be right, as in, "You should be or act this way." I used this tool as a weapon, either on myself as condemning judge, or on others as critic. "Should" is a heavy word that appeals to some abstract universal law. "Should" thrives like bacteria in egg salad sitting in the sun, even in our family conversations. Using this word on others is actually impersonal, judging by a set of standards rather than personal response to who we are in working out a relationship.

In exchange, I learned the value of another tool, the loving "could." I could do what I had done before, but I could also try new or lost desires and strategies. I began resurrecting my list of dreams that had previously vanished. "Could" allows for the development of a menu that presents options which are open to creative alterations. "Could" equipped me to quit looking at the past and what it "should" have been, and to consider what the future could be. Could replaces should. The one exception is when we make a promise; we should always do what we promise. This is life under covenant instead of law.

This talk of should and could may feel like it is a long way from a theological conversation. But it is exactly where the issues get stowed away in our lives. We live under the "shoulds" of all the people that surround us. Voices from churches mandate specific should-behavior. Our culture wants us to be politically correct, which is to live under a should-law. Emotional fashioning is a constant feature of cultures of should. Should is the cage of emotional constraint.

The term "law" can refer to the force of any external set of standards and ideals that seek to conform us so that we lose the rareness of who we are. This kind of law is devastating for relationships because it is heavy and brings guilt, shame, and the fear of rejection if we fail. We go into hiding. Thus, we do not grow in freedom, in the natural interplay of loving relationships with God and others who love us. We do not learn from our mistakes; we bury them.

"Could" is a term for life with the Spirit, where a possibility is just that, one of many options when pursued with loving companions. These confidants populate our journey and allow us to develop as exceptional persons. They encourage us to explore the possibilities from love, rather than neediness or recklessness.

But the possibilities may look wild to some, as Jesus experienced when he was called the friend of sinners. U2, the rock band, lives a life that honestly explores living with questions, and they "still haven't found what they are looking for." All the while, they appreciate the ability to live from the love that brings fidelity to their personal relations and music. They live and sing from what "could be." Some people merely live in the wreckage of their stormy past.

My storm wreaked havoc in my personal world, leaving devastation from my failure to love and be loved. Fortunately, it also cleared the mist I had lived in. I could now see that I had lived in the fog of a lonely valley, dreaming about the sun above. But I still yearned for someone who would accept me unconditionally, and whom I could accept without fear.

In April 1998, I lost nearly everything. I lost my job at church, as often happens, when a new senior pastor took up residence. I lost the house and property I had been restoring. I lost a wife I still loved, but she loved another more. I lost my kids, as their primary residence was with my previous spouse and the man she was soon to marry. The lightning bolts were intense, decisive, and devastating. I was displaced. I was angry. Loss was eating me. Unsure of what my future would hold, I survived on the gifts of generous friends.

I am divorced by the choice of another; this has profoundly shaped my personhood. I would never have chosen this label of brokenness for my kids or myself. No longer could I think of myself as better than anyone. Branded as a vulnerable, imperfect person, I faced the challenges of singleness, ex-hood, and contentious co-parenting. I had to find my own way through the wilderness of Christian nicety as a highly-educated, forty-year-old divorced father of three very young kids, with a library of over 12,000 books, and little else in the world.

But a new hunger gripped me: a desire to *live* all that I had been educated to believe about loving and being loved. This made me a proactive listener-to-God in a way I had never been before.

By grace, while attending Regent College for a post-doctorate, my journey of transformation made a significant step upward to becoming a person who has discovered post-storm sanity.

On a particularly bad day, I was depressed about finances, my writing was not going well, and I was discouraged about the divorce proceedings. As I prepared to drive to Seattle to see my kids, a graceful invitation stopped me and changed my life, like a first glimpse of spring sunshine.

I was invited to coffee by an Australian student who listened with absorbed attention to my flash flood of woes. Then she queried me. She asked me if I remembered the children of Israel in the wilderness. I said yes. She asked if I remembered how God took care of them. "One day at a time," I replied. She asked if I had enough for that day. I did. "What about tomorrow?" Probably. Then she asked the big question that changed my life: "Can you trust God with the tomorrows that follow, one day at a time?" The force of her question hit me like a gust of wind, blown all the way from the Garden of Eden, where Adam and Eve walked trustingly with God one day at a time. Her question stunned me. She was asking if I was ready to live as though I have already been loved, and to trust in that love, in a practical day-by-day turn of the calendar. I felt like it was Easter morning—as if anything could be possible if I could learn to trust in the personal love of the One who knows me.

Following our conversation, I put this personal greeting on my cell phone—Easter Morn. Repeatedly, it reminded me that in the early morning hours after the storm, a possibility exists of being birthed to a new kind of love that comes unexpectedly, changes everything, and brings a clarity and relief to how one gets up and greets every morning.

The hope of the Resurrection is of highest importance, for it is the ground of an anthropology that says I am only complete as a person when I come to deeply trust this Other Person who is for me, with me, and loves me. That full person, Jesus, can do what other humans cannot: love us to death and life again.

I had loved the best I could, but had not been loved. That was not enough.

I had grown up learning to love, but confused love with fear. That was not enough.

I wanted to love and be loved.

While at Regent College, I wrote a searching poem, exploring this clarifying investigation in dialog with my four-year-old daughter, Anlya. It was a roadmap check, establishing a cadence for discovery, but the best was yet to come. I still had miles to go, but already the storm was more than clearing ground; it was creating a new continent on which to abide.

Read this poem as an alternating dialog between father and daughter on the threshold of life.

TO LOVE AND BE LOVED

One day the question came to me,
Daddy, what must I do to be happy?
    My Anlya dear, there's a thought that's grand,
    And one often asked throughout the land.
Shall I travel near and wander far,
Go by bike, plane, or car?
Will I find what I want in far-off lands,
Or running on beaches of pure white sands?
    You would see the world is a wonderful place,
    Full of frontiers, fun to chase.
    But you would find an ache hard to erase,
    Missing your friend's and your family's face.

Shall I settle down by the fire,
Spend cozy nights at home to retire?
Should I work in the garden, plant flowerbeds
At home with my family for long years ahead?

    You would enjoy a comfortable household,
    A place where your loved ones you could enfold,
    But a heart yearns for adventure, to wonder and explore.
    Home is good, but your spirit needs more.

Shall I play with the neighbors and climb in the trees,
Throw a ball in the park, fly a kite in the breeze?
Will it make my life happy to play many games,
Watch lots of movies, carefree of what I became?

    A life filled with laughter is a marvelous thing,
    Learning to dance, to swim and to sing.
    But fulfillment is added when you find fruitful work,
    The kind you wake up to, ready to perk.

Must I find a job, save money in the bank,
Fulfill my part and move up the ranks?
Does work fills the gaps and make life worthwhile,
Give a sense of meaning and make my face smile?

    Finding what you love to do is a worthy thing.
    Knowing you have helped can make the heart sing.
    But making a living can consume your life;
        balance you will need,
    Invest your time in contentment fine,
        which money cannot feed.

Should I think great thoughts and go to school
    to prepare this growing mind,
Memorize the things most wise and see what I can find?
Will a four-year degree fill me with glee, or should I go beyond,
Become a doctor or lawyer, fulfill a vision fond?

    Learning fills a certain yearning that opens creation wide.
    Understanding helps you move in order to survive.

But filling your head can feel like lead, and you may fall asleep,
You need some entertainment to make your spirits leap.
Music and dance could fill my nights and make my spirit pour,
Maybe a night at the opera, a symphony, or concert roar.
Should I flood my hallways with music always,
Delight my days with matinees and first-class Broadway plays?

    The performing arts can touch our hearts
        and make our dreams to soar.
    They give us wind to fill our sails,
        and make visible what many ignore.
    But if we spend our waking hours watching someone else,
    We slowly lose our worth;
        and all our hopes, through neglect, we squelch.

Then should I dream like a foreign queen,
    and imagine a happier life,
Where days are filled with feasts and folly, never a thought of strife?
Can I hope for days when I will have children,
    and we shall travel and play,
Or live securely without money worries, but just relax all day?

    Dreaming is fine to pass some time, to set a higher course.
    We need some vision to guide us, to fuel our energy source.
    But we must not neglect the past too fast,
        forgetting our life's deep roots.
    The history that brought us here
        is the trunk that brings Spring's shoots.

Will delving into the past fulfill,
    knowing from whence I have come?
Can my family tree bring joy to me,
    as I learn of mothers, daughters, fathers and sons?
Will the stories of travels, triumph, and loss
    fill me with purpose today?
Can I hope to feel glee when my context I see,
    how it shaped me to be this way?

Remembering is a worthwhile thing
    which helps us understand.
It helps to make clear our patterns here in relating to our clan.
But days of detailed digging can put cobwebs in your head.
You eventually need to get up from your desk
    after you have read.
Then shall I run in fields of gold and climb the rugged hills,
Swim in rivers rushing cold until I've had my fill?
Shall I ski the slopes and fulfill my hopes to sail upon the seas?
Can I ride a horse and set my course wherever I may please?
    The spirit of adventure will breed in the open air.
    The wanderlust will feel a new gust
        in the wonderland out there.
    But take some time to read reclined,
        tucked in some comfortable chair.
    Explore the worlds in other's minds;
        their thoughts and adventures share.
Shall I sit and read, on the library feed,
    to explore the thoughts well-told,
Adventures in the Amazon, and mystery novels tenfold?
Will I find some joy, hearing of girls and boys
    who live in far-off lands,
Digest the encyclopedia, read all my eyes can stand?
    Cover to cover there is much to discover
        in pages filled up over time.
    Pictures and poetry, sonnets and mystery,
        follow where you are inclined.
    But don't waste your youth on merely book truth;
        you'll grow old while you're still young,
    Let your legs stretch while you're fit and can catch;
        age will move up the rungs.
Shall I find happy truth in preserving my youth,
    maintaining the Spring of my years,

FACE to FACE

Keep my skin softened, muscles use often,
    and forget about danger's fears?
Will it help me to live if my tender years give
    me wild adventures to tell,
Throw caution to the tide, and not try to hide
    from the urges that beg me set sail?
    Childhood's bliss is not to be missed,
        but lived with a natural joy-play,
    Life rushes on away from this dawn, so don't ever waste it away.
    But growing old is a journey, enriched as you come and go.
    Find friendships that make your life full;
        these make fond memories grow.
Then growing up shall be my goal, to develop beyond a foal,
To find some folks to share a meal, and fondly feed my soul.
I will find a settled way, like those with plans outlaid.
Will this finally find my happiness made?
    Growing old is what we do;
        it does not matter what you choose.
    It is a pleasure if you spend your life,
        not fearing what you might lose.
    But it's what you put in that makes it good,
        starting in childhood.
    Then give your praise throughout your days,
        doing all you knew you could.
Then I shall give my life away, and care not if I work or play,
I'll do the deed and give the hug, tuck each child in and pray.
Will I then know the happiest way, giving love my days so long?
Is this the best that I can hope, fulfilling life's final song?
    To love is indeed a noble thing,
        enough to make the heart to sing,
    It is the purest giving thing,
        and gives you more than you can bring.
    But being loved is needed too, to know that others care for you,
    It makes houses homes, and gives joy when life is through.

Then I shall drink the love of all, and fulfill my journey's call
 I'll find the friends to feed my heart until my curtain's fall.
I'll blow my worries to the wind,
 and forget the things on which my hopes were pinned.
I'll take the kisses and the flowers, when my love I win.
 To be loved is sweet as honey fine,
  and fills the world with songs through time.
 It's a fruit in season, fully ripe,
  to taste and nourish and move to rhyme.
 But, dear one, listen well,
  to love and be loved is the dance fulfilled.
 Happiness is in living, giving, and receiving all;
  and then the heart is thrilled!

I wrote this poem because I wanted a better life for my kids. In the confinement of niceness, I had missed the exploration of what loving looked like, and what it meant to be a full person. I recognized I had started on the wrong foot. Life is to be lived with invested passion, not in the fear of missing the mark. I regretted discovering so late in my life how mistaken I was to understand sin as merely breaking the rules. I now believe the gospel will never make sense in daily living until we gain new perspective to understand what it means to be persons in relation, as well as understanding what threatens us, which means to discover the relational nature of sin.

Chapter 5

The "I" in Sin

"I've been too honest with myself; I should've lied like everybody else."

—*Manic Street Preachers*

"Should we all confess our sins to one another we would all laugh at one another for our lack of originality."

—*Kahlil Gibran*

"Without love the virtues become vices. Truth without love puffs up and is evil. Beauty without love is seductive and empty. Goodness without love is moralism and a façade."

—*Dwight Friesen*

OUR GREATEST ANXIETY IN life is the fear of rejection. On a day-by-day basis, we hide our faults and play a game of hide-and-seek to evade the eyes that see and slough us off like sunburned skin. And, on the flip side, acceptance is our deepest desire. We are wired with a longing to connect and belong. Caught in this tension between fear and acceptance is the struggle of life: an energized attempt at wanting to survive. But in the process, we become imprisoned by not letting our true self be seen. In the hiding, masking, medicating, and denying that veils our humanity, we become inauthentic. Most of us cannot be truly honest with ourselves or others. We are numbed into this poverty of soul, naively hoping to gain what we cannot trust people to give us—acceptance just as we are. This separated, scared, synthetic life is the experience of sin: born in the seed of fear, forged in the anxiety of daily disappointment, and finalized in our sense of individual security that needs no one else. It leaves us as our own worst critics, or subtle cynics. Also, it hones in on the flaws in others.

The I in sin seems to reach out and poke us in the eye. It carries an accusative sneer that always wants to point out what is failing in our fragile existence. It is a word that flows off the lips of those who claim to want to heal us, but are just as ready to damage in the diagnosis. But who gets to write the book on sin? The TV evangelist? America? Traditionalists and their lists? Our own accusing consciences?

To believe in a God of grace, we must silence our accusers, and listen anew to the divine voice. When addressing the issue of sin, God's desire is to heal us, not squish us under a colossal thumb. God desires to love in a way that overcomes our state of hiding as we recover from the distress of life's challenges and our own self-interested natures. Do you think God gives failing grades? Do you act as though God gives scores? Does your intuition hint that God wants perfect children, or honest and zesty ones? If you have in your head a story about God that makes you afraid, you are probably a victim of monster projections of God intended to scare you. Jesus got most angry at those who cast these manipulative caricatures.

Some will say at this point that God is holy and cannot be with miserable humans. "Look at the Old Testament and see the wrath on sinners," they will say. But God creates a good world, intends to bless all the nations through Abraham, and keeps sending crazy prophets to bring God's children home. God's holiness needs to be seen more as the intense desire to make all things whole. Holiness is for creating wholeness. At times this does bring discipline, but only to set things back in loving order.

The message of grace is that God has already accepted us, and loved in the most sacrificial way possible. God acts restoratively to overcome our neediness. Sin, on our part, is not welcoming God's acceptance. It means we reject God, and walk on alone. Sin is the saturated life of experiences and possessions that numb us in our disconnectedness. Sin is simply a state of living that impersonates love, but turns love on its head by making it about self-care instead of about other-care. No one wants to give up sin because, in the moments of satisfaction, it feels so good. But we are numb to the gnawing that eats at us. We desire to simply be loved, but rarely are we satisfied. We feel lonely, insignificant, meaningless, and insufficient in exposed moments, but mostly keep these monsters at bay, though they still buffet us.

I got a spanking on my first day of kindergarten. I was innocently chasing two girls for the sheer fun of being with playmates. Without trial, I was ushered into what seemed a torture room called the foyer, and disciplined in a way that seared my soul, but left little memory of pain. This experience made me shrivel and want to be such a good boy I would never get in trouble again. Both a blessing and a curse, it kept me out of trouble, but restrained me from chancing the risks involved in loving. It made "not doing" more important than the wonder of discovery.

We all get training in how to think about sin or being bad. In my home, there was not much talk of sin, but we kids knew what not to do. In trying to avoid the appearance of evil, we often stop doing anything courageous, and end up as listless puppets. Sin, and the fear of getting in trouble, can make life a game of hide-and-seek. Many shameful secrets end up as skeletons in the closet. As we hide our embarrassing-snapshot-memories from view, our secreted seclusion chisels our soul to dust.

Everyone has a top-ten blacklist of sins arranged in priority from worst to excusable. Later in life, I learned that not everyone works with the same menu. My parents disliked alcohol and its effects, so it made my sin-list. Thus, I avoided even tasting it. Consequently, I was thirty-two years old, and living in New Zealand, far away from my parents, before I sipped my first beer. I could take it or leave it. But with the sweetness of a shot of Bailey's Irish Cream, a Kiwi friend seduced me to explore other "sinful" libations. This act of drinking did not seem to be sin. It became a taste of heaven in my morning coffee. I understand that alcohol abuse tragically devastates many families. But one cannot quarantine the planet from potentially harmful substances. Drugs can either heal or harm, depending on whether they are used or abused. I prefer to connect the term "sin" to "abuse." This still affirms the "use" of the same act or substance as good in a loving context.

For instance, the tongue can be used or abused. Unleashing forbidden words was certainly not acceptable at home. During a few short weeks in elementary school, I dared to swear with friends, but I never risked trying it on adults. It thrilled me, like waving a Fourth of July sparkler as a child, a swirling flash in the night that lasted a few seconds. In moving past that bit of daring, you might say I became a bit vanilla with my speech. I became harmless rather than expressive, missing that top layer of sweet, dark sauciness. Boringness becomes its own kind of sin, a loss of self in playing it safe. My form of "goodness" was a state of fearing trouble that was not good at all. That is the sin of inauthenticity.

Enter now the hottest topic, too sizzling to bring out on the table for fear of lighting up the night sky. Sex was not a topic of conversation at our house, so mine was a basic National Geographic education. Friends-in-the-know carelessly slipped out clues in casual comments: "Do you know what the F-word means?" The black-and-white lessons of my junior high health classes analogously reduced the thunder of what was like a night's experience at a rock concert to a boring black-and-white program. I was very interested in the dance of life, but it all seemed strange and foreign. The sight of nakedness was magnetic, mostly because of its forbiddance. The entire out-of-bounds nature of nudity made me more interested in beautiful female bodies than in physical acts. Sin looked like a chocolate factory for adults only, where grown-ups set the rules to keep the good stuff for themselves.

I thought of love as attraction, but the act of sex was never a part of that pull. When I was twenty years old, a girlfriend mentioned "making love." I was naively but firmly convinced that this phrase meant nothing more than acting lovingly. Admittedly, in my world, sex was always tainted with the sinful. Like a will, it was not to be opened until later in life, and then you would find out what you got. In my world, love and sex were incompatible languages. Loving and being loved had little to do with this dangerous physical world of human bodies, and possibly making babies. In my world, most sin involved misuse of the body, or even the desire for sex itself.

Sex and sin are deeply intertwined in the apartments of our minds. When we think that right now millions of people are sexually active in rooms somewhere out there, our sin filters might kick in. Are they married? To each other? Are they both willing partners? Is one infected with an STD? Many are embarrassed even thinking about what others are doing. I *wish* the cautious reserve to think about sex stemmed from a deep respect for the gift of sexuality. But I fear that, ever since Garden of Eden events and the birth of shame, our viral thinking still views the physical and pleasure-seeking side of being human as contaminated, not in God's will. But sex is a good thing, a real thing, a connecting act. What we do with our sex drive is a significant question. Do we hold it as a gift, or as a self-serving treatment for our hungry and wounded souls?

Like alcohol, we know that we can abuse sex, as well as joyfully participate in it. But while many cultures publically drink wine with their families or beer with friends at pubs as a healthy participation in life, in America, sex is generally associated with selling something, including sex itself. Our culture has no "public honoring" of the private coming together of human bodies. Its many euphemisms are smeared on city walls, and stain the conversations of the brash. Against the bareness of our culture's presentation of sexuality, Bono, from U2, speaks of the mysterious in sex as most alluring. That mystery is an honoring and cherishing in the act of tender touching that makes it holy and precious.

Gary Smalley's concept of five love languages helps us recognize that everyone communicates love differently. Physical touch is one mode of expression, and intercourse is only one dialect of the many modes of touching. Physical touch, as I conceive it, includes whole domains, kingdoms, phylum, etc., of expressions that fall within this arena. In a world of fear, we are increasingly cautious about how our physicality is interpreted. Like tribes losing their last members, and with them the memories of a language and a history, we are losing a language of loving touch for fear of a lawsuit.

The sterile world emptied of sexuality is no safer than the expressive world that cannot stop talking about sex. Editing out sexuality is simply living in denial of who we are. The love-starved outcome of this tragic form of human existence spreads like cancer. Sin simmers in the emptiness. Victorian morality taught us that cultural clampdowns are merely external. But hope for the future begins with loving connecting in the heart. Good marital sex therapy begins with relationship repair, not techniques.

I love Old Testament professor Ian Provan's idea that there is little difference between prayer and making love. Both are deep expressions of intimacy. Both are celebrations of covenant love. But while I wish for a life of praying without ceasing which seems spiritual, it feels needy to think about sex every day, as I do. I sense the natural hunger and the nobility of constant prayer, but am challenged by the subtle, apparent selfishness of habitually desiring sex. Giving *and* receiving are the dance I desire. Life is about the mutual conversation.

Although sex is meant to be an expression of love between two people, I am aware that I desire to feel its pleasure. The "I" in that statement casts an ominous shadow over how seriously sex can be considered an act of love for my spouse. I value the image of reciprocal gifting that makes it an act of love.

I know that, because I am a male, I cannot imagine or speak for women who are afraid to walk alone at night or in secluded places. Sexual abuse stains this conversation. I fear that most women see men as takers. Sex can become a sinful expression of robbery even in men who love their wives, but demand sex as a right because they lack an understanding of love's mutuality. Sex is not the sin; the sin is disconnection from the other as a loved and respected person.

One of my professors taught that sex is the core metaphor in the Old Testament. All the violations of Israel and Judah are portrayed in terms of adultery, engaging in sexually expressed worship with the gods of the nations. If we turn about-face, we see Yahweh's language of worship is also sexually infused, but with the character of fidelity. The Song of Solomon in the Bible is called Holy of Holies by Jews because it is the book where men and women live wholly before God in physical bliss with God's blessing surrounding them. A healthy life of caring spirituality must not surrender our sexual being to mere appetite or abstinence. We must redeem the sacredness of touch.

Left unattended, our youth-oriented, consumer mentality runs wild. The playful-sanctity of sex diminishes to a mere recreational act. Sex becomes an active ingredient in people's preferred addictions. This ranges from pornography, on one end of the spectrum, to retail therapy safaris where people attempt to look attractive in pursuit of feeling loved, at the other end. Both are pseudo-attempts at connection. Without learning how to engage in healthy relationships, we cannot help but default to our culture's siren song to fulfill individual desire.

We cannot cure the world by telling them they are thinking about sexuality inappropriately, or wrong for thinking about it at all. We all are a bit confused. The condemning scheme only furthers the destructive doctrine that God is against sex. Many believe that God has mobilized the church to control the rest of humanity. Too many just wish that we could all be ignorant of sex until married. Although these are all myths, they permeate our culture.

If we are ever to redeem sexuality as a viable part of our life of loving, it will be through becoming adequate practitioners of healthy, mutual, loving, physical expressions that fuel the relationship to last the journey. As long as our culture caters to individuals pursuing selfish needs, the opposing judgmental voices will focus on sex as the chief sin. But when we learn to communicate compassionate self-giving through the physical, sex will be a chief love. Sex alone can never create a lasting loving relationship, but it is a vital symptom of one.

I now take you back to the menu of mischief that shaped my sense of sin. Many creative explorations that got other kids into trouble were expressions of a cuisine mostly foreign to me. For example, only once in my life did I take a few puffs of a cigarette. I disliked the taste and the feeling it created on my tongue. It produced a dry sensation that I also experienced eating pancakes. I still am not fond of pancakes today. As a pre-teen, I was pressured into this act in the deep woods behind my house so that I would not tell on the other smokers. Their thought was that my smoking would incriminate me as well. I had no health concerns back then, but was worried about getting in trouble. I endured the emotional bruise of being a sinner, feeling dirty and disobedient for having failed to keep the good-boy rule of not smoking. Rule-breaking weighed upon me, though I was naive as to why all the rules were there. Sin became associated with being caught. For many, this is still their dividing line: everything is ok as long as you don't get caught.

Some menu items jumped off the page to grab my attention. Rock-and-roll was forbidden at home, but in my teenage years I rebelled a trifle, and fell in love with the Beatles, the Beach Boys, and the Moody Blues. Music began translating my dormant emotional life into musical moments of escape. As I heard musicians radically breaking boundaries, my emotions awoke. But I still feared I might transgress, so I limited my musical repertoire's expansion. I bought into the belief that sin began in the emotions, and then became action. The cure? Guard your emotions! Avoiding sin meant avoiding emotions.

What a tragic lobotomy this diminishing of emotions creates! What an impossible myth: to think that we could even control our emotions without fear driving that agenda. Thus, fear imprisons us. No action in our lives is void of motive, which is to say, *every* action originates from the emotive part of us. I now believe it is sin to lose our emotions or to think we should. In fact, even "rational" people are motivated by the hidden fear of being wrong, hence wanting everyone to be rational like them. Their deep well of emotions is a pool of bridled passion. They think protection, security, and a controlled future will help them face their anxious thoughts about what might go wrong in the coming day's events. But they are wrong. Once we begin to insulate ourselves, we will forever want more refuge. "Be reasonable" equates to "Think like me so I don't feel the insecurity of your difference."

Craig McNair Wilson, the creative guy who trademarked Imaginuity™, says that reason stands at the door of our mind like a pair of sentinels and asks, "Who goes there?" The sentinels function as agents of fear. Reason, acting from fear, screens the horizon to make sure we stay in the safety zone and do nothing foolish or fun (or emotional). But no living person performs a single act without a motive. Reasonable people are dominated by fear motives. And motives are the moving components of the emotive world. Though it is said, "Men are rational and women are emotional," see how advertising works, and think again!

Millions of highway signs and seductive marketing strategies hit the bullseye of a man's emotional world through sex, sports, and big toys.

Some of the most difficult clients I work with as a therapist are reasonable men who think they need to be in control. Their stuckness often originates in religious-based fear, abuse from childhood or work situations, feeling poor, or protecting wealth. In the end, they are controlled by their fears, and petrify in their pontifical positions.

The world of "thinking rationally" owned my mind for years. Intellectually, I could like sinful people, but felt little compassion or empathy for them. I had no desire to be a sinner—whatever that might be for me—so I avoided the activities on the sin-list. I lived with that line in my mind that divides the human race between the good and the bad. Either we are on the good side and can referee those we reject, or we stand on the failed side and feel our own shame in the pronouncement: "unworthy of love." But grace relieves us of being the gatekeepers. Fooled, as by a mirage of a dangerous world, we engage others judgmentally. We cannot be a neighbor in that stance, for we make them our adversaries. This is the fruit of rationality when fear wins.

A realization dawned that while I was avoiding the actions of sinful living, my new game was to judge everyone else but never look at myself in the mirror. Hiding my symptoms from sight made the disease of not loving "go away." But this scheme did not sit well with me. Of course, not many were inviting me into sinful play; I was a Goody-Two-Shoes, and would have spoiled their fun. This whole world of concealment imprisoned me in a constant threat of exposure and rejection. The need to be carefree and trusted greatly appealed to me. Sin looked fun, but feeling loved for being good felt better. Tragically, even this was life under the moral microscope of judgment.

Illegal drugs are still absent from my story because of my need to be good as well as because of the obvious risks. But I have learned compassion for those who habitually indulge, and I feel a sense of the tragedy of their plight. I also learned that judging is as devastating a sin as most other sins. Jesus's greatest resistance was against judgmental religious leaders. Paul's letter to the Romans is his surgical attempt to remove judgmentalism from the church. When those who judge others do not practice love, their criticism is further tainted with the hypocrisy of looking holy, but void of the compassion of God's holiness.

Idolatry, replacing God with any other object of affection, is the central sin in the Bible. Sin is about a loss of emotional and relational allegiance. But still today, most people seem to think the great sins have something to do with sex. Our culture has lost its language for idolatry, for it cannot conceive of a life of fidelity to an invisible God. Hence, most people—including Christians—live with rampant unidentified expressions of misplaced affection. We have exchanged quality relationships for possessing objects. This is an epidemic of our age.

One day as I was listening to Simon and Garfunkel, a line hit me from their song, *The Sounds of Silence*: "'Fools,' said I, 'You do not know, Silence like a cancer grows.'" The image of a world of disconnected people silently missing each other became for me an image of sin as cancer. This is the cancer of relationships, where uncontrolled noise disrupts our hearing, and invades our interrelating. The "tumorous" presence of addictive activities and substances dominates and erodes the health of all our relationships as we set other priorities. When someone says "I don't have time for this relationship," all I can hear them say is, "This is not a priority for me." Worship in our culture is about getting our priorities focused, and living in a corresponding

manner. What is of greatest worth to us wins the invest-
ment of our time and attention. Silence can be the mere
head-nods we give to people who should be of great value
while our energy goes elsewhere.

This does not mean that people living in silence are
bad. Silence can be a gift. Unfortunately, guilt, shame, and
distraction often force people to retreat into isolated islands
of refuge in their minds. But sin solidifies in souls living
in separation. Like moss growing in damp and cool places,
our unsettled emotions eat away at our memories of friendship with steady decay and a sense of detachment.

Rather than sin being an action, I see sin as relational
distance. It is the breakdown resulting from everyday acts
of neglecting to nurture love. Sin is the ruptured relationship. Living in sin is living disconnected. Once separated,
we manifest hurtful and disrespectful actions, not to mention the subtle absence of the healing actions that foster
connecting love. We slide into hiding from each other
because we fear the other's judgment. Thus begins the self-
medicating pursuit of new passions to ease the pain of loss.

We often confuse sin with its symptoms. Sin is relational separation. Its symptoms show up as anger, hatred,
revenge, and other emotions of harm against the other.
These attitudes are born out of the painful distance that now
exists. We are blind to the deeper issues. We may treat the
obvious signs of breakdown, like getting upset or avoiding,
but leave the disease unhealed. We may judge estranged
spouses for making poor choices as they head off alone into
the night. However, policing their nightlife will not heal the
marital relationship.

The enormity of the confusion between sin/separation
and sins/symptoms enlarged for me when I began to think
about churches that feel unsafe. Insecure churches have
halls where the walls peer with inspecting eyes, scrutinizing

with unfriendly x-ray vision, while latex gloves snap in preparation for examination. They do not manifest the love of Christ. They are only the body of Christ in name, not in character.

All humans have to deal with the fear of rejection and correction; it is the basis of peer pressure. When judgment permeates a church culture, no one can show his or her real self. Religiosity within a fear-based culture profoundly fosters the cancerous sin of separation and isolation. If a person deviates in a small way from the unspoken rules, they experience great fear that an unfriendly "Christian" critique will follow. The risk of being found out nudges one down the path of covering over—like an invisibility cloak— to ward off the dreaded day of criticism and shaming. This is a tragic view of atonement (meaning to cover over sin) that is moved by fear. Covering up to "keep the peace," and "sweeping under the carpet" are secular wannabe equivalents of atonement because they do cover over failures, but in festering invisibility. Biblical atonement covers with love that heals and redeems. If Jesus's atonement means anything, it is that God's love heals by covering over the brokenness of our humanity. He deals with violations through forgiveness and reconciliation. It is love-motivated, laying down a life to save a relationship. This overcomes the human inclination to hide like Adam in the Garden of Eden, inaccurately thinking God would be mad. Atonement is love in action to rebuild the web of relating.

I know that most churches do not intend to be unsafe. Unfortunately, it is a natural effect of the "cancer" of "keeping up appearances." Many congregants don a mask of propriety to deflect attention from the spreading cancerous growth of judgment. Looking "lovely" becomes a duty-mask, a thin covering; but fear of failure becomes the operating system.

I understand why many people choose not to go to church; they do not want to endure the climate of conformity. They fear exclusion by the alienating culture of the church that does not know how to embrace them as they are. Similarly, I know that good-hearted church people do not intend to convey this message. It is a stalemate of eternal proportions. Until we rethink the nature of sin, we may find ourselves continually living with narrowing options to be "good Christians," and become less authentic in the process. We need to function as chess knights who move outside traditional unbending lines.

Fear always looks for evidence that something is wrong, and usually finds it. Thus, anyone who enters into congregational life risks rejection and manipulation when attempting to be real. In every act of speaking, it is possible that there subtly appears in the mind of the observers a red "A" or some other branding symbol cast in indelible ink. Humans judge so quickly. All too easily, the "mature" authorize themselves as "protectors of the truth," and hence, become "accusers of the brethren." As they point out errors in actions or beliefs, fear creeps in. Fear carries a magnifying glass, which burns when the light is too intensely focused.

We all tend to think the best of ourselves. But when I reflect on my life and thoughts, I recognize that my intentions are not always loving and pure. How can they be? I am susceptible to enlarging sinful symptoms in others to make myself feel better. If I set aside my fear-spectacles and put on new grace-of-God glasses, I begin to feel God's uncomplaining acceptance as God sits with me and envisions all the loving possibilities with each situation I encounter. Grace does not turn a blind eye to breakdowns, but it never gives up looking with the hope of redemption. That means to bring people back home, or to find healing from loss and pain. When I do not pay attention to the voice of Jesus,

I am overcome by the voice of the Accuser from behind, shaming me for who I am, and blaming me for my faults and failures, not to mention the disasters in others' lives. Condemnation moves into the convergence zone where storms are born, and the world grows dark and dangerous as emotions become charged.

Our natural human default is to move out of the zones of conflict, and live a life of performance to gain acceptance. This produces a life with an "I" focus. Our concern becomes focused on the unholy trinity—me, myself, and I: How will I get out of this one?

As a rambunctious five-year-old boy in the garden of childhood, I could not know I was stepping into the eye of a tornado when I tried to find peace from the storm by attempting to be good, which became my life's focus. If only I had known, it would have been healthier to step out of that emotional storm. I might have begun to be a free spirit, filled with courage and wonder. But that would take decades to rediscover. The winds of authoritative voices swept me inward to self-protection. In that safe/unsafe position, I was truly engulfed in unfreedom. That emotive location was the self-in-the-prison of the protective mode, alone with the "I" in isolation.

The seclusion of "I" is not a physical apartness, and it is not an emotional separateness. It is more than physical distance, for we can love those miles away. We can never escape feeling for others; even hatred, though it feels like distancing, is a tragic form of emotional connection. The I-am-alone mindset is life caught in the illusion of being on our own and possibly unsupported. Our deep need for love compels us to employ coping strategies to address our assumptions that we are alone (and relationally, we are). We tool up for survival by developing masks, avoidance techniques, and other escape mechanisms. Many parents attempt to preempt their kids from creating coping tools. With the best of intentions, they involve them in sports and music to avert them, through controlled activity, from exploring temptations, rather than teaching them to have open, honest relationships. All these management measures end up trapping us in the downward spiral of coping. The whirlwind of fear propels us down the road of dysfunction, the road more traveled.

Sin is not about people being bad or breaking the rules that God sets. It is living separate from an embraced relationship with the living God. This happens because we do not know God as good. We default to living with a persistent fear at the center of our soul. This natural inclination decenters us, and fractures the very relationship intended to heal. But the great call of the New Testament is to not live in fear, worry, and anxiety. It is to that whole spectrum of fear's family, that moves us into fear's dysfunction, to which we must now turn.

Chapter 6

Fear's (Dys)function

"Many of us crucify ourselves between two thieves
—regret for the past and fear of the future."

—*Fulton Oursler*

"Fear is a darkroom where negatives develop."

—*Usman B. Asif*

"He who fears something gives it power over him."

—*Moorish Proverb*

"We have nothing to fear but fear itself."

—*Franklin D. Roosevelt*

IF PURSUING LOVE IS the central appeal of the New Testament writers, their most important thing to avoid is fear. But try to find a theology book with a chapter on fear. It is a missing chapter. Yet one can hear the penetrating advice of Jesus: "Do not live in fear, little children, for it has pleased my Father to give you the kingdom" (Luke 12:32,

65

paraphrased). Living in the kingdom means not living in fear. Our ancestors have tried to reform the church because of the fear of heresy, failure, irrelevance, seeker-sensitivity, and a host of other fears. But if fear is operative in our theological recipe for change, it will spread like yeast and spoil the whole, rather than give rise to the kingdom of God.

Ultimate love is a concern for others without losing care for self. Ultimate fear is ultimate concern for self.

Jesus was fearless because he was motivated by love. He was not afraid of death, loss, or failure. He could live without sin because he lived in an unbroken love with his Father and the Spirit. Without relational distance, and with love, sin is dispersed. We can positively understand what God is seeking when we see human failure not as broken rules, but as broken relationships. In dealing with sin, God is restoring us, not in ourselves, but within God's shared life. Righteousness, holiness, justification, and all those other positive goals are not measured performances to see if we pass. They are terms to depict a life that breathes fearlessly in an intimate love that compels us to act with a resultant love.

Fear is to be void of love for others. This void is not an emotional vacuum; it is motivated by a concern that only knows how to protect ourselves. When this protective self-concern called fear extends to every human, we get a fractured humanity that we try to keep under control. Society is a term for people, managed under a common set of rules and administration, who do not really know each other, but live impersonally under an administration of power. A fear-based culture manages the behavior of self-protective humans who lack a theology of love, and live in a shadowy theology of fear. This is a life that avoids being seen, caught, or hurt—life under the radar.

If we live in the fearfulness Jesus wanted us to avoid, we are likely to end up needing something like MapQuest to get back on track to the life he envisioned. Many think Jesus came to save sinners from hell. While this is true, it is not his focus in the gospels. He came to reunite humanity back to his Father because they were in a Far Country and needed to come Home. His goal was to redeem those who became enslaved to their addictive solutions, to heal their lostness and loneliness, to guide them back into the Forever Family for which they were made. He came to feed the hungry and heal the sick, to bring wholeness. All this restorative work is the just outworking of his Father's love for a broken world.

Helpful theology makes all the systemic aspects of human sinfulness clear. It makes visible that we are out of harmony with a relentlessly loving God. It reveals that God sees the problem, and has acted to reverse the curse of separation. The church is to be God's research and restoration service to deal with the sickness of the human soul.

Entire blocks of cancer research buildings in Seattle, Washington, attack a major health threat to our nation and world. People are willing to invest heavily in a cure. I propose that a cancer in human relationships is also at epidemic proportions. We live in a culture of fear and polarization in which we mostly fear rejection, but are riddled with many other forms of insecurity that immobilize our lives.

I see a critical need to identify sin as a cancer that functions out of fear. Sin is the separation and disconnectedness of our personal lives. Absolutely everyone is born ignorant of God, so we default to caring chiefly for own needs. As a result, fear becomes as natural as breathing, in that it is our self-focused motive for survival. What feels more crucial than our continued existence? Nothing else motivates us like fear, as we raise shields of protection to ward off perceived danger. One side of the coin of fear is self-protection, which, if sustained long enough, translates into being stuck in self-interest. The other side of the same coin is that, when we are afraid, we lose awareness of God and the needs of other people. Searching for safety and peace, we filter the constant chaos of people pushing us and pulling at what we think is ours. Defensiveness develops into cold, stone walls, excluding friend as well as foe. The resulting silence feels like peace, but is merely a gnawing emptiness. As our detachment develops, the cancer spreads.

If we do not hear God's voice, it means the connection is broken. On our side of the divine relation, we are born into a separated state: not as bad people, just disconnected. But on God's side, we are known and loved. Nothing can separate us from God's love. From God's vista, each of us is the object of love even while we are still ignorant and hostile toward the very idea of God.

I have come to understand sin as the absence of what God desires: loving presence, and nonjudgmental acceptance. Jesus heatedly confronted the religious leaders who judged and condemned. The Son of God was most interested in spending time with sinners and tax collectors as their friend. Trying to be "religious" is a setup for the very sin that Jesus still resists: self-idolatry. Many religious people try to be good, but Jesus's Christianity is a lot more about being honest than being good. Sin is more about broken relationships than broken rules. Branches survive only when connected to the Vine, as John's gospel illustrates. If we are going to survive, we need sap to "feed our vines" a lot more than we require stakes to hold us in place.

People used to share family life in their homes; now we are disintegrating into living apart from one another, even in the same house. Whether we live in spacious homes or tiny apartments, many of us prefer retiring to our own space. We elect lives with an "apart-ment" quality, hoping to quarantine ourselves from inquiry and hostility, but end up sterilizing our lives. We are amazingly blind to how our health is sustained by our connectedness, the nourishment of loving and being loved. Until we see sin as a disease that divides us through fear, we will live under its powerfully motivating influence, a mothballed menagerie.

The roots of this new perspective go right back to a close reading of the story of the Garden of Eden. In that habitation of beauty and provision, God created a place for abundant sharing and caring. Adam and Eve lived a life of joy-filled dependence on God. Like innocent children, ignorant of the trouble they would encounter later in life, they were naked and did not judge it as wrong. In fact, they judged nothing; only God judged what was good, and that on the basis of whether it fulfilled the goal of love. God also provided the possibility of a forever-fellowship eating from the Tree of Life.

In the next dramatic move, an enemy cunningly invites the couple to eat from a different tree, the Tree of the Knowledge of Good and Evil. In eating its fruit, they are told, they will become like God. Here we must pay close attention. Notice what ability suddenly appears after eating the fruit. It is the ability to judge between good and evil. One instant—unable. The next moment—their eyes were unwrapped, not from shut to open, but from innocent eyes to keenly and fearfully discerning eyes that judge. Imagine, one minute you are with God and accept his wisdom; the next moment is a tragic leap away from God to stand in a place of independence. We think independence is good, but here it is loss of connection and belonging. One bite, and the rollercoaster takes off; humanity is screaming with a new force in their consciousness. Now they can judge, and it is not good:

I am naked! Therefore, I am *ashamed*.

She did this! She is to *blame*.

God might be upset! I must hide, for now I am *afraid*.

The great theological point here is that, in rejecting God, they now fear being wrong, not trusting God's gracious judgment as they now question God's goodness. Rejecting God replaces confidence with concern for consequences. Fear supplants faith.

The biblical story depicts this point as the beginning of a new phase in history: the era of independence is unleashed, profoundly resembling the teenage move to autonomy. There is no separation of *physical distance* here; God is always present and still comes for a morning walk with them. Their rebellious move is one small step for a person, but a giant leap for humanity.

Adam and Eve move from dependence on God to a place of independent judgment, thus creating *relational distance*. Rather than aligning with God, they take a giant step away from God. This means they suddenly make choices with a new priority, asking, "How will this choice affect me?" Adam and Eve become mentally castled-in by judgmental, fear-based attitudes of self-interest and self-protection. They develop coping mechanisms to defend themselves against any person who questions their actions and attitudes, including God. Sin feels secure when well-armed in the darkness.

Fortunately, this is not the end of the story. Another possibility called "interdependence" describes the adult stage in life. When two adults agree to let go of their separate power, to work together for the good of both, they exercise interdependence. Those who seek mature relationships must recognize we all work with different expectations, which necessitate choosing "both/and" instead of "either/or." We cannot lose ourselves for the other, or expect the other to bury their desires for us. We need to be willing to seek what honors both persons. Faith is dying to self by giving ourselves to another. We die to the independent, sinful, separated self. We are made new as integrated persons in Christ. We acquire renewed relational identity: we are sons and daughters of the Father, brothers and sisters in Christ, and children adopted by the Spirit. The life of faith is not about going back to the Garden to become dependent on God as little children. It requires a life of showing up ready to cooperate in a spirit of community. We finally eat from the Tree of Life in communion with Christ as we share his life. That is what communion is all about.

Recognizing sin as a loss of connection taught me that I cannot be in a loving relationship when I blame, shame, or need to be right. The loving way empathetically hears the commitments of the other person, maintains self-respect, and tenderly charts a course that respects both. The power of sin is weeded out from the garden of love.

You may be asking whether I have taken sin seriously enough. What in the world does this "separation stuff" have to do with the cross of Christ, who died for human sinfulness as the greatest sacrifice?

First, the cross is God's act of love on behalf of separated humanity.

When God sees conflict, he does not run from it; he runs to it. The cross is God seeing sin, honestly assessing its death blow, and engaging it. Because of love, God runs toward conflict to overcome separation. God never denies the actuality of human self-judgment, self-centeredness, or destructiveness. God's Grandness is in acting from a love that sees the human disease, yet judges like a doctor: from love, acceptance, forgiveness, and a desire for healing. Then God intervenes with the healing strategy that fits our disease.

Second, God overcomes separation with reconciliation. Whatever offence has occurred toward God or any other person, intentional or unintentional, a character trait or circumstantial, God identifies and redeems in an act of loving forgiveness. God is the ultimate public servant.

Third, when we look at the cross, God does not intend us to feel shaming guilt. However, healing guilt recognizes a wrong done, and moves to restore what was lost. In the message of the cross, we are intended to hear God's invitation to a life of interdependence. We are to leave our independence behind, just like when we marry and join ourselves to another. We are summoned to be mature, loving adults with a childlike heart—without fear: full of wonder, natural trust, and desire to connect.

Fourth, God is not interested in controlling us, but wants to launch us to breathe the new air of the kingdom of God on earth. When we live in this place, we honor God's name as Father, enact the heavenly life on earth, receive the supply of God's daily nourishment, awaken to the forgiveness already offered (which is to be extended to others), and are kept from self-satisfaction and relationally cancerous activities. We learn to cooperate within God's kingly humility. We become kin, and share in the kin-dom of God as a diverse family, united by a love not our own.

But fear causes self-centeredness. Fear is the default of our humanity, the core motive of our emotional system that wants to protect ourselves. Get someone to fear rejection, pain, or loss, and you will quickly awaken their self-concern. Fear is not bad as self-care, but becomes cancerous when it takes over our lives as the chief operating system, continually asking, "How will this affect me?" as an overcautious scout of our lives who goes before us.

People are unaware of the impact of fear in their lives. As a professor and speaker, I sometimes employ an exercise in which I ask participants to turn to a partner and say, "I am not afraid of you." This is generally easy for most, even among strangers. Then I say, "Tell your partner what you think about them." That is a little hard for some. Next, "Tell your partner what you think about yourself." Self-disclosure is generally more difficult. Finally, I ask the participants to consider telling the other person their deepest, darkest sin. This is most challenging as deep fear emotions begin to emerge regarding what the other will think. By this point, my listeners usually feel fear's impact.

Years ago, I did this exercise with a group of about eighty third-generation Chinese students in Vancouver, BC. One student, upon hearing this challenge, raised his hand from the back of the room and said that he would share. He came down and revealed the events of a weekend with his girlfriend at Whistler, events for which he had genuine remorse. When he was done, I asked the group if they had more or less respect for him for being honest, transparent, and vulnerable. Everyone affirmed more respect. Even in a culture of "saving face," which lives from fear and wears masks as much as Americans do, fear was abated and sin was disarmed. Everyone in the room felt it. Other-centered love embraced, and changed the climate in the room. Love does not overlook sin or forget it; love extends forgiveness to heal.

Healing theology never isolates an individual from what is going on in the family, congregation, or group. Sin is not an issue of the individual alone, but of malfunctioning relationships. It is a dissonance that resists God's desire to create resonance with humanity.

When a church cannot maintain a culture of love, it becomes a dysfunctional family. Functional families have an ability to change with the transitions of life. But dysfunctional families are unwilling or unable to change, and

stuck in power structures that mummify. Even one controlling authority figure can lock everyone else in a rigid place.
Dependents suffer in the forced silence, whether inflicted
from above or perpetrated elsewhere. When people feel the
bite of pain and loss, they medicate to mask their aches.
This gives rise to addictions, various unhealthy forms of
coping with life's challenges. The range of self-medications
is vast, from the observable abuse of drugs and alcohol, to
the less obvious use of religion and money. All are used to
anesthetize a devastating array of emotional traumas.

Addiction begins when we desire a medicating substance or practice badly enough to be willing to lie to keep
the supply coming. The lie may be small. The medication
may be honorable, like church, work, or exercise. But our
chosen medication is merely a symptom of missing what
we really need: love. Something is missing, and we fill the
loss with our "cures," but the cure becomes the disease. Alcohol has addictive properties, and some are predisposed
to its effects. But in a healthy, loving family with nothing
to cover up or recover from, it loses its power to control in
an environment of support. Not all addictive processes are
triggered by the substance itself. Addictions can begin quite
innocently with good elements in our life.

Subtly, yet drastically, the moment we lie to cover up
our addiction, separation sets in, and we live within our lie.
"I need to work this much to get ahead" is one example of
a seed of deception to feed the drug of success. Those who
share the lie are codependents, maintaining the deception
to keep the peace. "Oh, he doesn't work that much" is a
common statement dismissing an eighty-hour work week.
In the acts of covering and enabling, we define ourselves
as codependent. This is how addictions function like sin in
our lives: they prejudice us toward self-interest, and disconnect us from honesty with others. This phenomenon does

not know class or economic distinction; it is color blind, and affects both genders. Addiction is an equal opportunity employer, and employs on the spot without references.

For example, someone missing physical intimacy with their spouse may deal with their loss in an unhealthy way. Instead of communicating to their spouse about their desire, they may use the instant gratification of technology to simulate the real thing. But the imitation stimulation will not heal the relationship; the exact opposite will happen. Their desire for sex is not bad. The longing to get their needs met is natural and understandable. The problem is in their self-seeking prescription. The cure is killing their relationship.

One day, I found myself buying used books and putting them on the shelf before my former wife knew I had purchased them. I later realized from this experience how addictions work. I wanted books because they made me feel smart and respectable—my identified need. I hid the purchase to protect my fix. The hiding was a lie based in fear. I came to see that absolutely anything can be addictive, because it is more about what we need to hide than any "thing" in itself.

Addiction is about living a lie, even regarding little things. Loving and being loved is being honest—yes, even about the little things. This is not a call to fully disclose everything to everyone; it is paying careful attention to relationships that matter. As my wife the dentist often says, "Only floss the teeth you want to keep."

My sin in my first marriage was in trying to be good rather than collaborative. Focusing on being good, I turned to the resources of my past: books and friends. But I neglected to really hear and work with her to make her life fulfilling. My education and employment were a higher priority for me, and I am sure she felt it. She wanted to be fulfilled, and she was not. I do not even know quite what her fulfillment would have looked like, but it is now a question past asking.

The life of loving and being loved must be oriented in friendship. In our personal relationships, whatever is not done to nurture friendship is sin because we use people as objects, and it depersonalizes them. Sin destroys friendships. But I do not need to become a judge of myself, always second guessing. We need not live in constant fear that we will unknowingly violate others. That focus causes us to fall into a trap that is another form of self-centeredness. We simply need to honestly respect the other for who they are without losing respect for ourselves.

In my journey of discovery regarding sin and not living under its power, I have found that my goal is intimacy with those persons who matter to me. Escaping from intimacy is the self on fear-medication. It is not good to be alone, as God said to Adam. It is a funny coincidence that "id," placed in the middle of the word intimate, is intim-id-ate. "Id," the selfish "I" in the heart of sin, violates intimacy with our significant others. To be intimidated is to live in fear.

I still fear rejection by people I do not yet trust. I know I am not alone in this; even in my struggle, I sense that I am standing within the presence of triune grace, whose light reveals in order to forget nothing and heal everything. Love uncovers the solitude of sin.

We try to heal ourselves in unhealthy ways that ingrain our disease and spread the epidemic of addictions. We can understand this whole process of human breakdowns only if we move beyond thinking that addictions are merely about harmful substances, to discover that we all have addictions that diminish us and fracture our relationships. We all are grounded in fear, and nurtured in addictive patterns;

that is why something is missing, and it is significant. Our holy hope is to live free of fear's power in a life of honesty that can reconnect us as persons.

Chapter 7

Addicted to Love

"You do anything long enough to escape the habit of living until the escape becomes the habit."

—*David Ryan*

"Habits are first cobwebs, then cables."

—*Spanish proverb*

"We are so accustomed to disguise ourselves to others that in the end we become disguised to ourselves."

—*Francois Duc de La Rochefoucauld*

SPREAD THE NEWS! THEOLOGY is a hope-filled engagement with the story of a God who is on a mission to restore the family of humanity to come home. This God is not addicted to having songs sung to entertain and satisfy the triune song of harmony. This Extravagant God is in the business of taking broken lives and relationships, and making them whole. This Truthful God is not delighted in being Just and Right to show us we are wrong and pitiful, but rather, desires to be true to the love that is God's very nature and serves his beloved family in sacrificial self-giving to bring humanity back into his arms.

The God revealed in Jesus does not favor the top students, but notices every child, every marginalized person, all who have been robbed of their dignity. God does not hate any: rich or poor, male or female, civilized or barbarian, outcasts or in-crowd, young or old. This God sees the frailty and vulnerability of each person, even though we are all distracted—like teens in spring—from a loving face-to-face relationship. Health is faithfully living within God's love, and becoming a unique person. Illness is any state of living in a life that fears rejection and builds callouses to endure the abrasiveness of the masses that press against our dignity and make it hard to see ourselves as beloved ones.

This calloused coping is the journey of addictive, fear-based living. Granted, this is not theological language; rather, it is a practical terminology that reveals the patterns that plague humanity. In order to clarify where we are going, we need language that can keep us from being stuck in old thinking, and guide us to new linguistic tools that serve our relating to God and one another.

People can keep calling our brokenness sin, and say it is our nature, which may be helpful for some. I still maintain that we are all sinners, but also hope to give a depiction of addictions that shows how sin works in our daily drama. I believe the cross of Christ has addressed our sinfulness by loving us just as we are. But this is not like a wave of a magic wand. In the death of Christ, we see a profound invitation to be honest about who we are. Why? Because the event of the cross declares that the Father intends to remove any belief in us that God is against us. God takes all judgment to God's self so we will know we are accepted. God wants us not to be afraid like Adam. Fear makes us dishonest and distant. When alarms go off in our head that we are in trouble, our deepest inclination kicks in. We hide, creating a pseudo-self; that is the core of addiction.

The deepest message of the cross is that we are loved into the life we were missing. We are already accepted and embraced before we do anything. We cannot condition God into loving us; we have been loved unconditionally. In our release of the fear of judgment, the power of addiction is undone. We then find freedom simply by being with the One who loves us—not in an imagined autonomy apart from God.

Addictions come in more than thirty-one flavors, and most of us have our favorites. We all love their sweetness. We mostly use the term "addiction" to describe someone else's out-of-control habits. Conveniently, as with ice cream, we are kind to ourselves, making excuses for our need to "treat" ourselves. Just trying to cope, we use substances and activities to balance our emotional accounts, and fill our emptiness with a taste of "heaven." Unknowingly, each such practice is a bite from hell.

Many are made aware of the world of addictions by hearing the painful news of family or friends flailing in a web of drugs or alcohol. How ironic that I stumbled onto addiction therapy after beginning to explore why churches are so dysfunctional. Researching addictions, I discovered that beyond addictive habits and substances, there are often addictive personalities. Further, families can be addictive systems, comprised of entangled relatives unable to function freely. At an even higher level are addictive organizations, including businesses, government, and even churches. Finally, I found that even societies can have addictive structures. But how does this awareness help find a road to health?

Up to this point, I thought relational problems were to be wrestled through by the person with difficulties. But with new eyes, I saw that entire systems are often sick. I found that addictions are merely symptoms. People act badly in response to their emotional surroundings. Controlled people will become rebellious. In most relational ecosystems, the deeper dysfunctions continue undetected as people stuff their dissatisfaction. But features of dysfunction are present anywhere people hang around each other. Eventually we develop patterns of "self-medication" to numb the pain, loss, and conflicts within our story.

In my adventure, I wrote a paper called "The Church as a Dysfunctional Family" for a course in Pastoral Counseling. At that time, addiction literature was all quite fresh. I found helpful concepts to understand and tell the stories of why loving and being loved is so challenging. But I also found God as a more-than-adequate family. I discovered the brilliance of trinitarian theology, the study of God's family life, to be a baseline against which to assess how we as humans mess up. Nothing shows up failure like seeing something done well. But the Trinity is not just a model for us; it is the family for whom we were created. Fail there, and every aspect of our lives feels the consequences.

God is not addicted to anything because there is no fear in the triune life. But we as humans have some core needs that set us up to be unsuccessful. We want to be loved, to feel accepted. This is so deep that we give up ourselves to be what others want. Sacrificing authentic self-revelation feels necessary to be liked. We give in to peer pressure in order to be accepted. We try to keep up with the neighborhood in order to be recognized. It never goes away until we die. It is even worse for those who live in the spotlight: politicians, professors, leaders of all sorts.

The most powerful addiction in America today is an addiction to acceptance. We want love, but we lose ourselves, paying the price by burying our authenticity to get a cheap form of acceptance that feels like love, but is an imitation. Love is freely given; conformity costs us our lives. But we are addicted to feeling loved. We do not know the real thing, so we accept the game of deception to get our fix of feigned acceptance. We fear the rejection, which is the power that drives us to the dark side. We do not realize that the life offered by God is given specifically to address and rescue us from this addiction, and give us what we truly crave.

This whole pursuit of studying God in relation with humanity is tricky. For one, it has been severely abused by people who want power, and prey on people looking for acceptance. Yes, they use peer pressure to cause conformity, and the cure becomes the poison. All addictions come from the sales tactics promoted from fear-based strategies, whether by pimps, dealers, or preachers. "You need my product or you will not be happy" is the lie to which our desperation blinds us.

Second, the way people often talk about this God-human relation can easily default to a mere study of the human, and neglect hearing God. We humans like to hear what is in it for us. So people run to God to hear what is new to get control of their life. But this is the thirst of a self-love that is not real love at all. They come to suck what can be taken, hoping to ease their challenged lives. They miss the authentic engagement that nourishes and heals the human spirit.

Some people want the best of both worlds, integrating theology and psychology to describe and heal the God-human relation. However, "integration" is not a term I favor in this conversation. One reason is that the attempt to reconcile these two different systems of thought, keeping their different assumptions in place, means that neither is really honored on its own terms.

Psychology is a science that asks, "What does it mean to be human, and how does this human function?" But it is a pursuit limited to human observation of the thinking, feeling, and behaving of an individual. It requires repeatability rather than the uniqueness that marks humans.

Theology, on the other hand, focuses on God's revelation rather than on human experience. Its best researchers ask, "Who is God, and how does God function toward humans. How does Jesus help us to see what a fulfilled human looks like? How were humans created to live? How might humans respond as those created for companionship?" But the integration project begins in a wrestling match to decide where to start. Should they begin to study the human by hearing what God says, or focus on what human observation tells us? Psychology has to maintain the stance of an objective observer with a clinical distance. Theology enters into a dialog of exploration, and hears the stories. Who should define the nature and health of persons in functioning relationships? Which really gives you knowledge of the person in front of you? You cannot be uninvolved and involved at the same moment.

"Contextualization" is a better place to start. That means to see one thing in the context of another. Words only have specific meaning in sentences. "Mom, what does this word mean?" She replies, "Give it to me in context." When I stand to look at specific aspects of any person's life, I want God's interrelating life to be my frame of reference for understanding them. Are they just a body with a brain, or are they a beloved person? From there, I explore how therapeutic activity might function to fulfill God's purposes.

As humans, we all have our different experiences that bring profound diversity to what we think life should look like. Our life context is unique, and should be valued. But there is always value in listening to the manufacturer. Contextualization, in this case, is to position ourselves to hear the original intent of the Creator, and then to live reflectively in the light of that intent. Like riding a bike, it has a discipline that opens the doors to enormous freedom. And that intent is to live in love and face-to-face relations.

Attempting to understand either theology or psychology is challenging because both speak a new language unfamiliar to most of us. We are likely to read in assumptions and world views alien to the authors. But if we can learn to read each on its own terms and traditions, we will understand them in context. Science wants to study us as objects. That is fine if we do not assume that there is nothing more. Theology wants to study us as beings who live best when relating to God and one another. That is alright if we do not forget that we live in a material world to which we must also pay attention. Science speaks to the lower, objective nature of our existence, and excludes subjects (personhood) in its study. Theology speaks to the personal nature of our existence, and humbly includes the material aspects. It sets the context for the discussion of being persons in face-to-face existence. Theology creates the context for understanding our humanity as whole persons.

Theology also sets the context to understand how God speaks through the Bible to our addicted, dysfunctional families. How does God's functional life heal our human brokenness? By showing us what the character of a self-giving love and an interdependent community look like, and inviting us into one. A diminishing number of people get close to this kind of experience in their family. But learning this kind of participation is the hope of humanity.

How would the world change if we interpreted the Bible in ways that specifically impact the particularities of family life with God's love? For most of us, our default is to do what our parents and TV have shown us. We speak the language of our past. We live from reports of days gone by that become scripts that write our futures. We live our habituated patterns, and are stuck in reflections of happiness and love; we are defined by what is behind us as we drive through life looking in the rearview mirror.

We need a fresh start. On the day of Pentecost, everyone heard in their own language the mighty acts of God. The Old Story came through a new experience of hearing God's voice. This occurred as the disciples, through the Holy Spirit, communicated God's unknown character—loving, creating, reconciling, and redeeming—to a diversity of needful ears. Our task as therapeutic theologians, humble parents, and friends is the same. We all need to know we are loved just as we are today, with hope for a richer, shared life tomorrow.

What does that life look like? I define personal health and wholeness by observing the community life of the triune God. Specifically we need to learn how the Father, Son, and Spirit interrelate. Sounds crazy, right? If we allow God's activity to give meaning to our language, it may break us out of old patterns and expectations.

For example, Jesus's holy acts give "holiness" a Jesus-filled meaning, especially his acts toward the unloved. As the friend of sinners, Jesus brings his wholeness to the broken. He ejects any idea of holiness as being about separating from sinful people. Instead, he infuses the term "holiness" with a new meaning by embracing the rejected with God's transforming love. Jesus embodies holiness. He gives the word meaning in action. When we come face-to-face with this kind of transformation, it will reshape us with a new vision through a new, sculpting language. "Be holy" becomes a call to embrace others, not to judge.

We must not allow love, peace, freedom, and other terms of relating to become abstract concepts. These are concrete modes of interaction that define God's relational involvement with the world. He invites us to stop wobbling through life guided by our many blurred meanings based on faltering human experience or wishful abstractions.

We are best served in living a healthy life by allowing our assumptions about human fulfillment to be critiqued. We cannot just use other blunderers to give us their opinions, though they may have valuable stories. We are invited to allow our game plan to be reviewed and redirected in the light of how God lives and interacts. We are not to go on alone, but with a Guide who wants to see us live fully.

If we are to be doctors of the spirit, we must allow God's kind of love to ignite our basic motivation, from which our communication and actions flow in correspondence with God's. For the Jesus of the gospels, love is sacrificial giving, rather than our assumption that love is getting our personal needs met. Peace, gifted by the Spirit, is the fullness of an embracing presence, not the absence of conflict. Freedom, extended from the Father, is a way of being with—not away from—others. We need to see these divine Persons at play in the landscape of the biblical story to add texture, depth, and color to every enacted word, enriching their recipes. Only then can "love" not be a cheap imitation that is our core addiction. Authentic love brings face-to-face, heart-to-heart knowing and being known.

But we have compressed the voluptuous grapes of God's words into shriveled raisins bereft of their full exuberance. Jesus rehydrates the life of words. This process of letting Father, Son, and Spirit resurrect our communication enables us to share therapeutic realities that correspond with God's language and life. "Family," though a biological term, implies a connectedness brought by the Father "from whom every family on heaven and earth derives its name" (Ephesians 3:15). God establishes a family and gathers, sustains, nurtures, and empowers it. God invites us to translate these movements of caring as the context of our life stories. We do not need to get God into our lives; we need to get into God's family life. But we are often stuck in our own tragic dramas.

Marriage is a desperate arena in which we ask what other-centered love acts like. Might love be expressed differently in Seattle than in Rome, or in caring for the broad diversity of wives, children, and husbands? Undoubtedly. God is sensitive to those differences, and intentionally improvises on his themes of love. Tragically, marriages often become monotone. Living a daily-recycled rerun, couples cover their needs with invisibility cloaks. But God's creativity expresses love anew every day to the differing needs of those God loves. Marriages get caught in mirage scripts that miss the reality of spouses hearing each other. But God pays attention, and constantly translates love into new contexts. Successful marriages learn to play along, translating the language of the kingdom of heaven into our native tongue.

We must not let our culture's language of control violate God's original language of love. Everywhere, the "shoulds" of correctness keep us in watchful check. When we are with transparent lovers of God, the "coulds" of possibility enable us to feel free to love and enjoy all our neighbors. But when we are with selfish brats, we get disgusted with them. It is so easy to develop judgmental eyes that see from a point of view that condemns the dysfunctions in others. How amazing that we so easily turn a blind eye to, or excuse, our own dysfunctions.

Like all those systems that put us to sleep in school—such as the skeletal, muscular, and cardiovascular systems—metaphorically, the addictive system is core to our personal being. Much like our skeletons, we don't talk about the addictive system, which is out of sight, so we never notice it until we feel the pain.

As previously confessed, I innocently discovered my own addictive system. We become aware of our system with the emergence of specific symptoms which we call addictions. My favorite addiction is to books, which seemed so blameless, so innocent. I did not figure out the problem right away; likewise, it will take time and patience to discover your own addictions. But they leave a mark, an existing bruise from which we never fully recover, though we can grow in amazing ways when we learn to engage our addictions.

First, we need to see how easy it is to blame the thing to which we are addicted: "The drink made me do it." We scapegoat the alcohol or whatever drugs we let pollute us. In some cases, the substance itself is a factor in the destructive process. But we would not pursue our fixes if the deeper diseases of pain and loss were not poisoning our emotional systems.

Second, addictions are only powerful because we use them to address genuine human needs: coping with aching loss, emotional or physical pain, and the ever-present confusion of our lives. All humans medicate, ranging on a wide spectrum from a subtle chocolate attachment to a life of heroin abuse. We are all vulnerable in varying degrees, and will try virtually anything to help medicate our emotional bruises. The problem is that addictions do not bring healing.

My great surprise was to find that all good things may also become addictions. For me as an intellectual, books filled a need to feel competent and powerful. I still feel very small when I walk into bookstores, where literary giants laugh at me from the shelves. They all have been published. By owning their works, I stand on their shoulders and grow tall. If I possess their books, I add them to my team and we work together. Books filled my gnawing desire to feel worthy and competent as a professor. Addictive eyes see only the benefits, not the consequences.

Third, addictions are most dangerous because they damage relationships. When I found myself stealthily coming home, sneaking in with books acquired on my safari adventures to local used bookstores, I felt elated. When I browsed the rows of shelves, slowly piling bargain finds onto my sagging arms, it was every bit as thrilling for me as it would be to capture a great shot as a photographer, or bag an animal as a hunter. But when I drove into my driveway, the fear of interrogation set in. I sat there with my three bags full on the seat next to me. What would the over-cautious keeper-of-the-funds say? My response was, "Must think. Must hide." A brick was laid in my wall of protection, and the addiction was initiated.

My next movement was from the car, straight to my library, glancing both ways to make sure no one was looking, to quickly shelve my newly acquired books. No need to justify my purchase to my wife—ignorance is bliss—and she already thought I had far too many books (but I think that is inconceivable!). Books had long been my friends. The addictive process began when I chose to meet my need in an act of self-protection that I intended to be self-care. The unforeseen impact of my choice was like a guillotine's chop to the relationship. I fought to avoid someone weeding in my life, deciding for me what was important and what was not. This was a subtle move from the law of love into the turn lane of self-interest and the cul-de-sac of reclusion.

My fourth realization was that withholding information is living in denial; not telling is a choice to deceive. It is a white lie of nondisclosure. We feel self-justified once we start down this road, but the damage has begun. I was innocently and easily drawn by the goodness of books; they are glorious to me. For a long time, I was totally blind to the process of disintegration in the relationship.

Denial is a word that people who are in denial do not consider appropriate to describe themselves. They are just "playing it safe" or "holding their cards close." For most of us, denial works better as a label for others, to quarantine them. They are just "in denial." But we are usually blind to our own denial. It is a covering armor, attempting to conceal sections of our lives beneath a layer of protection. We are intent on removing the censure of persons who may disapprove whatever is Gollumishly "precious" to us. When we conceal our endeared things, judging eyes cannot remove the consumables or activities we relish.

Addiction is not merely about substances; it is the tragic, hiding game of holding our cherished hoard and, hence, losing relationships.

The moment we are willing to tell a lie, addiction is set in motion. We step across a threshold into the shadows. The shades of dishonesty may intensify from barely-veiled misrepresentation to pitch-black falsehood. Even a white lie has a dark outline; it is hiding something. We destroy relationships whenever our concealing protects habits we are unwilling to give up. Denial corrodes relationships, even in the subtlety of white lies.

Insight five shocked me: because they are socially acceptable, our most innocent and pervasive addictions are virtuous practices. It is easy to condemn the stumbling drunk or the ghastly meth addict. Their symptoms are so overt, no further proof is needed. But do you see the loss to a workaholic's family when the parent is consumed by work, leaving the widowed wife and orphaned children neglected at home? The children can tell you. Disregard produces feelings of abandonment in the deserted, while the addict is a virtuoso in self-justifying absorption.

Addictions are so much more subtle than merely overdoing controlling activities or taking an addictive substance. The widow-and-orphan effect is only one of many stages of losing someone in a powerless struggle. In advancing stages, addictions devalue and replace those we love.

If someone who loves M&Ms has a huge bowl of them out on the counter, and people say, "You are going to kill yourself eating so many M&Ms," and they respond, "What a way to die," I refer to that person as compulsive. In my distinction, their *honesty* means the habit is not an addiction, which would include hiding. Obsessive-compulsive people are annoying, perhaps, but not focused on secrecy. A red flag goes up the day they *hide* the bowl, and with chocolatey breath deny they are eating them. They step into the addictive alley of hiding and denying. Opening Pandora's box, they unleash a growing addiction. M&Ms are not the problem. The problem is their commitment to an addictive pattern to deceive. The process develops into an addictive attitude. Disguising unapproved purchases, questionable phone calls, or illegitimate meetings becomes a habit. Love is lost in this separating-from-trust movement.

And now, for the grand finale. Addictions are fullblown when we sacrifice relationships to save our "fix." When the workaholic is committed to the payoff of overworking—dreams of vacations, prestige, and money—they end up sacrificing their orbiting family relationships into outer space.

Ironically, exercise addicts cannot admit that their "health" activities are taking priority over family or friends.

Work is not bad, nor is exercise. But health must encompass more than just our bodies. Pursuit of addictive behaviors without concern for loss of relations is the vital problem. The plague spreads. The tragic addiction to self-satisfaction defaces relationships.

Those who are affected by an addict's pattern often develop their own disease, called codependency. They live within an addict's lie, defending the addict's actions and denying the damage. "It's not that bad" is the codependent's mantra. Convinced that the addict needs the fix to be happy, codependents often keep the "medication" supply coming. Codependents are also addicted—to acceptance. They want the addict's approval badly enough to ward off questions and sacrifice outside critics who used to be friends, resulting in a sick fusion.

Health in relationships is based on honesty and clarity of communication. When we reflect the life of God, we learn to trust by keeping promises we make to show love. But addiction creates an illusion mindset that replaces truth, and "loving codependents" believe they can hide and all will be well. Dishonest "love" is just fear dressed in drag.

Being addicted to acceptance may sound too subjective, but it is at the heart of peer pressure. With peer pressure, we want so badly to be accepted that we are willing to deny our convictions. We find ourselves participating in an activity we would otherwise reject, all to obtain acceptance. Why buy those jeans? Everyone else is doing it, and we want to belong. Peer pressure. Why take that drink when they taunt and you twist inside? Again, peer pressure.

Acceptance addiction is a most pervasive and refined addiction. Not merely a teenage phenomenon, it is deep in the culture of "keeping up with the neighbors." It is as widespread as the common cold. The cancer spreads as we surrender our identities, destroying ourselves and our hope for authentic relating, all to gain acceptance. This does not mean acceptance is bad!

Our culture is so addictive that we swim in it. Materialism is a huge addiction, not because "stuff" is bad, but because we use it to medicate our emptiness. We each try to gain status as we build our gilded cage. We are stuffed with stuff, missing what is truly important in life: our relationships.

Our way of life seems so normal until we get the notice that it is about over: the kids are fed up and leaving, the spouse is looking for an apartment, the friends don't answer, or the boss gives a final ultimatum. We pray that hitting the wall will never happen to us. The day-by-day mantra of "I think I can" mesmerizes us as we endure our routine struggles and miniscule rewards. This does not mean a routine life is bad!

Religion is deemed a good thing by those who believe, but it is not always good for everyone. For many, it is a prison of untruth. Religion has a tendency to focus people on conditions of acceptance, security, performance, belonging, and a host of other fear-based values. It becomes a hanging-carrot-pursuit that denies reality. One lives a lie of self-deception if they cannot be honest about their human imperfections, all because they need to look like a good Christian. If a congregation functions with a "don't ask, don't tell" premise in issues of anger, self-hatred, parenting, depression, loneliness, anxiety, and sexuality, that congregation may be run as a dysfunctional family. For many, church, mosque, synagogue, or cathedral functions like addictive dysfunctional families led by toxic parents on a power trip. This does not mean all religion is bad!

Criticizing religion is often a symptom of pain and loss. Because they resist relinquishing their own addictions, some nonreligious people criticize religion as a mere illusion. Examples of these people might be the playboy, the party girl, or the tough guy who won't listen to anyone. Pointing at others keeps them from looking at themselves, and distracts others from looking at them. But God's truth sees the addictions of life, and acts—not to protect the individual, but to heal the relationships of all involved.

Addictions immobilize healing. I concluded long ago that we are all addicts, mostly with socially acceptable or well-hidden addictions. People are tragically inauthentic, and unable to engage in honest conversations; that is a problem. It is hard to see our personal imperfections, especially the powerful consequences of our little lies. Change is difficult, and our flaws do not seem that bad. But how enjoyable could friendships be if we were relationally healthy?

Can we view the human situation as God does, and not merely through our own eyes? God sees us as children who need loving space to grow. He accepts us even with the dishonesty of our inward curving focus of attention. Even though our addictions alienate us from God, and hinder our capability to love one another, God has an unstoppable, restorative love. That is good news. We think being loved is up to us being loveable. We all try to appear good and upright, but keeping up appearances is tiring. We yearn to belong, and to be loved with childlike innocence. Tragically, we are seduced into hiding, like Adam and Eve, believing we will retain our innocence if no one sees our hidden secrets.

As humans hiding in our heads, afraid to be known, but still with a desire to love and be loved, we are run by a neediness-drive. Closeness is sabotaged while we pursue a treatment for our ache. Any fix we find only offers temporary relief as we chase our island-hopping life. Our search for self-satisfaction undermines the intimacy that could sustain our souls. This is not good news.

We all need unconditional love, but it confuses us. We are over-schooled in the assumption that we need to tidy up to be worthy of love. With each passing encounter, we must choose whether we will be honest, or pull out that polished appearance that conceals and protects. It is easy to use dancing lies that safely conceal more than reveal. But we could risk taking off the mask we think protects us. It requires risk to reveal our dirty truths; we call it "dirty laundry" because it is truth that we prefer to keep hidden. But it stops us from face-to-face intimacy with those we love. Can I be fully honest with everyone? No, but I want to try with the ones I care about. We have to engage in honest dialog in order to experience closeness. But authenticity is not our native tongue.

No topic is more at risk to be pushed underground than the arena of sexuality. Sex cuts to the core of us; it is inherently basic to being human. There is probably no aspect of our culture that is more prone to addiction than sex. We love it; we hate it. We are afraid of it. It mystifies us. Our sex drive is as innate as hunger. The media is saturated with sex to sell. But we do not *talk about sex* in a way that supports and dignifies loving expressions of sexuality.

We will never have all the answers, but we would benefit from respectful conversations. The empty silence provides fertile ground for addictive seeds to germinate. Married people are portrayed as the "haves," who are supposed to be the sexually satisfied rich. But multitudes of singles and marrieds feel like the deprived poor. They may see themselves as "have-nots," and resort to stealing by engaging in pseudo-relationships. Affairs, romance novels, sex magazines, soap operas, blue movies, and other placebo sexualities are replacements for authentic physical friendship.

People are hungry for love; they medicate with sex as the love-drug. But what are the side effects? Emotional emptiness comes the next morning, a symptom of being used or using. This can be just as true in marriage as outside. The act of sex becomes a temporary treatment to fill their aching desire to feel alive. But real friendship takes work.

More than any other voice, the church is uniquely situated to unleash and support an effort for healthy sexuality. This endeavor could be born from the beauty and elegance in the Song of Solomon. The intimate drama starts with simple delight, blossoming to shared gratitude before God. In the same way, we could affirm the gift of our bodies, educate in loving expression, and imagine a possible future where good sex is the fruit of a loving relationship, and not the means to achieve one.

I love sex. In public and in private, I try to value its sanctity as a delightful contribution to our human experience. In the movie *Yentl,* when preparing to teach Torah to his daughter, her father closes the curtains, admitting that he fears the neighbors more than he fears God. I, too, fear what the neighbors will say, because resistance in our churches constrains our conversations. The experience of hiding behind curtains means we live in denial where no one is safe. We are stuck.

Functional families are able to deal with change; dysfunctional families are stuck. Most people are not equipped to deal with life's changes. We stay hunkered down in foxholes originally intended for temporary protection. Like Narcissus, we become planted in our holes, rooted in our need to feel safe.

For many of us, our family feels normal until we realize how much we are afraid to talk about. With little overt conflict, it seems we have a "happy" family. One telltale sign of our dysfunction is what is unspoken in our conversations. Can you speak what you are thinking? Does it take courage? We are easily trapped in a comfortable silence that leaves the important issues in the locker room, but never serves them up at the dinner table. We think normal means healthy. But normal is merely *what most people are doing*. It is not necessarily functional, meaning healthy and loving.

A functional family stays unstuck even when things get uncomfortable. There is no question that cannot be asked for fear of ridicule. There is no disappointment that must be hidden for fear of shame. Opinions are allowed so each person can boldly present their concerns, knowing someone will hear with care-filled ears. No one person needs to have the final word; a loving discussion with respectful conclusion is the final word.

Rather than being driven by the popular question, "What is the right thing to do?" a new compass guides our exploration, asking, "What is the loving thing to do?" Love helps us finds a way for all confused and struggling voices to get the issues out and work through them. Love always considers the impact on everyone involved. When "being right" is the referee, a winner conquers and another loses. In actuality, this setup damages love between the parties so everyone loses. When love triumphs, everyone wins.

Addictive systems do not plague just families and churches. Any collection of people who utilizes a person or committee to define "right" for everyone else functions as an addictive culture. In society, when one race defines what is right, voices of other cultures cannot be heard, and entire societies are stuck. When one gender defines "true" knowledge, and is unwilling to share its power, the other gender is compelled to participate in a lie. When nationalism becomes a dominating force, nations may be stuck for centuries, and their addictive systems become normal. Honest revolutionaries are persecuted. People suffer. Natives die. Fear wins the day. Good news shivers in the writer's pen.

I am not a political activist. I am a theologian who believes that loving and being loved is a standard of relational health comparable to washing our hands and brushing our teeth. If we hope to change our lives, we must acknowledge that fear infects us. We must learn to wash away our fear like we wash germs from our hands, or it will infect each relational setting. The simple question, "Can we agree that everyone gets an opinion here, and no one gets to be right?" can sanitize for that conversation if all will agree to be open and nonjudgmental. We need more research on this!

We must crave freedom and health as preventative medicine. The human problem of sharing contagious diseases—like prejudice— cannot be blamed on any political or economic system. It is due to our ignorance about our many layers of fear and addictive systems. These become strong currents and undertows in our relational environments of home, church, neighborhood, and nation. Our desire to be safe and secure causes us to interpret all threats in a way that keeps us from understanding the other. Fear wins, we hide, and the world crumbles.

Churches talk about love, I talk about love, the poets and everyone else talks about love. But the love depicted in this book is absent from the fabric of our lives. Talking about love becomes a drug that fills our empty spaces. It is as though we are all addicted to love. We pursue every avenue of self-modification, stimulation, reenactment, romance, and physical contortion in our quest to find this holy chalice. But in our pursuit of this good thing, we ignore our shadow side—self-interest. Seeking love for ourselves, we come to the party as an empty glass waiting to be filled instead of as a treasured bottle of wine ready to be shared.

Love is grounded in gift. We love because God first loved us. Love is the risk God takes, investing without guarantee of return. That is our risk, too: our love might not be returned in a world stuck in addiction. However, if we do not receive and extend the grace of love, we are unlikely to break the binding bonds of fear. We will remain rocks that feel no pain, and islands that never cry. Conversely, love is its own reward, an antidote to the cancer spreading through our relationships.

People who are addicted to love aren't experiencing the real thing, but authentic love *is* possible. As we attempt to get our needs met, we will likely be blind to the consequences of our selfishness. I am not *against* getting needs met; this is the natural default of life. But I am *for* entering a life of tango, one where both the needs of another and my own are met in a climate of honesty. This is divine life, as captivating as the Aurora Borealis. You can experience this common phenomenon if you know where to stand: near the source, in a place without interference. The wind of the sun passes by the dark earth to create a spectacle of beauty and movement. In Word and Spirit, God's love ignites communities to luminescence.

I still function as an addict in situations when I feel fear, and my coping mechanisms begin to whir. But knowing what I now know, I have hope. When I live within love, I confess my fears, and can honestly buy my books. I can be unstuck, unstoppable, and unselfishly involved in conversations that embrace frail humans, and birth honesty. Love does not search for perfection, only connection.

Discovering our own tragedies and ailments is a process that clears the landscape, and lays the groundwork for us to explore. An adequate theology must usher us into a kingdom way of living that engages all of our face-to-face relationships and does not dismiss as "mere psychology" any part of what we have been talking about. Jesus came to bind up the broken in every aspect of human disability. Until we can acknowledge that something is missing—namely, a recipe and ingredients for healthy relationships—we will be victims of religious systems and political solutions that just further the problem. If we misdiagnose the problem, we will forever poison the patient. The good news is that what is missing is personal, and we now have a language into discovering how to be relational. The gift is given; don't just "believe it," but look Love in the face and say, "I am yours . . ."

Epilogue

I AM SITTING IN the living room of the Grünewald Guild,
a Christian arts community in central Washington State.
Just a bit ago, I listened to the founder of the community,
Richard Caemmerer, Jr., talk about the journey of discovering *who* we are as we create art, but in the end we need to
realize *whose* we are. I think we need both, but get snagged
on the first question. Ironically, if we do not go on to the
bigger question, we may not be able to answer the first.
Though the room is silent now, I am more convinced of
who I am as one who is loved, and loves to be with people.
Together we may creatively enter into the mystery of
whose we are.

This book has highlighted the need to be restored at
the level of our identity. For this pursuit, we must discover
with whom we belong. We need to dive into the silence,
and learn to hear the voice of God. We must acknowledge
the fear that is the great brake pedal in our lives. It is es-
sential that we address the consequences of being clogged
by all the mechanisms that we think protect us, but, in fact,
become our prison. In learning the mutuality of love, we

dive into knowing and being known in the unique beauty of each friendship.

This first book in the series could be said to be a study of introductory theological topics:

- sin (hamartology), human alienation, and brokenness,
- the Father (paterology) who loves us and sends the Son and Spirit,
- and human personhood (theological anthropology), including how we know and love.

Beyond these themes, this guide is an invitation to participate in the relationships that make us new persons.

I hope this book gives you fresh ears to hear the claims of God's deepest desire for all humanity. I imagine you might agree that the human need for love is the central thread that holds our humble lives together in hope of the good life, a godly life. Yet, we must confess there is little clarity on what love really is. Why is learning about love absent from the education process? Is there a reason the topic of love is avoided by contemporary philosophers? It is a haunting realization that the daily experience of love is missing for most people. Many think of love as a mirage, a chemical shot in the arm, or a form of temporary insanity in springtime. Something is missing.

When it comes to God, many of the people I meet are missing a life of love. For them, it is not enough that Someone is out there, somewhere, but is not here, touching and whispering to bring their lives into the tapestry of a life-giving story. A divine life may be everywhere, but what about here? God may know everything, but does God know me? The Creator may be all powerful, but does God have the ability to work in my life? These questions may echo a significant disconnect in the wasteland of many people's spiritual existence.

Many think of God entombed in ancient words carved in stone, or foreign words splattered on brittle scrolls now deteriorating in a faraway museum. Even a modern translation of the Bible may feel like a cryptic travelogue into antiquity. Furthermore, we are missing the triune God's vibrant presence because it is veiled behind the smoke of the burning issues. Debates rage in the church, and also shout at us from our to-do lists. The aches of our souls are engraved with unresolved feelings of pain, shame, and fear.

One northwest summer evening, at an outdoor party, my friend Bob commented about the emotional burden of a mutual friend. Our friend felt a persistent flood of inadequacy and shame for his addictive past, and the weight of the constant finger of divine judgment. He felt this weighty cloud as a tragic sense of the presence of God. Many people only know the critical God, an echo of critical parents, and the internal, unbearable reverberation of rejection that numbs the brain and deflates the heart. My reply to this picture of a condemning God was to ask, "Then why did Jesus say from the cross, 'Father, forgive them; they know not what they are doing'?" Jesus knows we don't get it, and are very imperfect! Jesus seems to assume something is missing from our side of the relation, but that does not stop his extravagant love. We are our own judges, and resist his compassion.

God is going to be true to God's character of love and forgiveness, no matter what we believe. You can shout at God all you want for being what you think he is like; God will not strike back. All the thoughts that fill your head will shape how you relate to God, but God will still be true to God's self. We will bear the consequences of not seeing the love that is actually there, but that does not mean God's enduring love is absent or diminished. We will merely experience the symptoms of our distracted adventures in missing the point. Our vision is likely to be diffused to the point of confusion.

You may think that God just wants us to get our thinking "right" about the topics that get preached about in churches. That perception is inadequate. This focus on holding an accepted position is called orthodoxy, which is translated "right teaching or beliefs." But maybe what we're missing in our lives are the right questions. Instead of asking, "What is the right thing to think, feel, or do?" theology might ask, "What is the loving way to be in this situation?" This could lead us to fulfill the goal of studying God to help us serve God and humanity. The first question sets us up to judge one another. The second directs us to find a way to work together. When we open our eyes to the deep currents of the Bible and the God revealed there, we see the text focuses on a process of loving God, neighbor, and self as a response to God's initiation. Isn't it strange that the Bible is a revelation of the way God loves humanity and acts to restore it, yet many who are outside the church think of Christians as self-interested, world-judging, and impoverished in enthusiasm for living the art of loving? The dissonance is telling.

The greatest act responding to what is missing in the world was Jesus's death on the cross and his resurrection. Too often, this is explained merely as a legal transaction where someone is guilty, someone pays, the account is settled, so let's get on with our lives now.

But the cross is not about a legal balancing of the books; it is firstly a proclamation of God's love. "But God demonstrates his own love toward us, in that while we were yet sinners, Christ died for us" (Romans 5:8). Upon seeing the cross, our first thought should not be about settling scores, but rather about the Father's desire to express love for us in our imperfect condition. The cross says, "I love you to death, and will let nothing stand in the way." The act fulfilled brings an unconditional love to fill what is missing. Its message is not about meeting conditions.

What is the most amazing proclamation of love that one could offer? The Bible says to "lay down one's life for a friend." Astoundingly, God gifts this love for enemies: for those who are alienated, distracted, self-reliant, and generally resistant. This love creates love by making the first move. The cross is a bold proclamation of acceptance that is intended to bring us home.

What keeps us from accepting God's acceptance? Missing an understanding of the depth of divine love. We think the Father will give us an F for not being good enough, or that God gives grades, so we do not want to sign up for the class. Learning a set of "right answers" or trying to conform to the expectations of Christians who seem so different from us offers a grim vision. Any interest evaporates when we engage people or a God who are only interested in changing us. Much more profound is the experience of falling in love, a knowing and being known in a growth trajectory that uncovers in a love-rich environment. We find a place of belonging. That is the gist of the gospel.

What is really missing in the church is not orthodoxy. Any *ortho* word is about getting life right according to a human set of standards. We need a set of *agape* words (the Greek word for unconditional love), such as *agapedoxy* (to think with other-centered love), *agapepraxis* (to act with other-centered love), and *agapepathos* (to feel with other-centered love). *Agape* is a love, sourced in God, that sacrificially gives to others as an act of compassionate other-centeredness. Disciplined into life by the delight of loving, these are the practices of those who abandon writing how-to books, rules, and regulations manuals. Instead, they write books of questions, such as, "Who is Christ for this community, and how do we share in Christ's love for these people?" "How is the Spirit calling us to empower and launch the gifts of Christ's body to serve one another and the surrounding neighborhood?" They lead by serving and empowering.

We need to move beyond what we do with head, heart, and hand (which are still the components of an individual in their own development) to enter into hugs which require the participation of another. Hugs get us out of our heads. Most Christian programs of growth, discipleship, and training focus on the individual in their thinking, feeling, and acting. But we must penetrate one another's lives, and participate in a knowing and being known that is the core of personal relating. Do you feel that your church leadership really knows you, and you know them authentically? Do you feel that God knows you right now and accepts who you are? Does this knowledge enable you to feel God's loving company in each part of your day? The Greek word for this participation in a shared life is *koinonia*. It is not a term for isolated moments of fellowship; it depicts living in a family of friends who are shaped by daily involvement. This loving participation should be the hallmark of the church's focus, an *agape-koinonia*. Used in a sentence, "Tell me about the *agape-koinon*ia in your church. How does the love of God sustain the church family with the love of God, and extend it as an act of unconditional love to those within your reach?" This is not about attendance, programs, dollars, or doctrinal stands. What the church needs today is God's triune voice to guide God's church, share the harmony, and improvise into specific contexts where we live.

This book was written to regain access to the operating system of the universe, which is personal, and to find that God's love is the language that keeps it functioning with wholeness. It is a necessary volume to expose that we are missing an understanding of personal relationships. We have bought into a façade that looks like the real thing, but lacks the deep connection. Even sitting in an empty room or church, one can come to sense that participation in community and meaningful relationships is more than physical presence. Deep relationships are a nurtured expansion of memory that creates anticipation for an ever-fuller sense of belonging, so that who I am is shaped by whose I am.

In Peter Jackson's movie rendition of *The Hobbit,* there is an interesting pairing of lostness and home. Home is not just a place, though that is helpful, but is a place of belonging. The dwarves are without their home, and Bilbo wants to help them get it back, even while he yearns for his own home. Lostness depicts being away from home. Thus, in this book, I have been playing at themes of finding we are lost, meaning not at home with God, whether because of fear, addiction, or ignorance. Now we must begin the adventure of finding that home is not just living where we are born, but discovering our place of fellowship, and feasting within a playful life of love.

Afterword

MY SINCEREST GRATITUDE TO Professor James Torrance, who years ago affirmed that trinitarian theology was relational. He asserted its exploration must proceed from the life of God made actual, to grace our lives as we share in the divine life. Also, I want to express my rich debt to Dr. Alan Torrance, who brings the highest level of intellect, the most vibrant passion, and the delight of living the gospel to all he does, including supervising my PhD, which explored the world of personal relationships. This journey of writing has been helped by a number of significant people. Alex Tamayo Wolf read first drafts and greatly honed my writing process as well as insisting this work needed to see the light of day. Anna Lyn Horky has spent countless hours editing and suggesting how to keep the work accessible and clear. My two daughters have read and given helpful feedback from a younger generation: Anlya patiently did this early in the process; Abby did a final thorough pass with "fresh eyes" to clean the text with brilliant insight. My dear wife Cindy reads, comments, and invites audiences to listen to a chapter at a time in ways that have smoothed out the text and added passion. I could not do what I do without her.

Afterword

I feel fortunate to have patient and capable companions to walk this long and thought-provoking road. I look forward to further conversations as I continue to develop further volumes in this face-to-face quest.

Further Reading

Anderson, Ray S. *On Being Human: Essays in Theological Anthropology*. Grand Rapids: Eerdmans, 1982.

Anderson, Ray S. and Dennis Guernsey. *On Being Family: A Social Theology of the Family*. Grand Rapids: Eerdmans, 1986.

Barth, Karl. *Church Dogmatics*. Edited by G. W. Bromiley and T. F. Torrance. Edinburgh: T & T Clark, 1962.

———. *Evangelical Theology: An Introduction*. Translated by Grover Foley from the first German edition of 1962. Garden City, NY: Doubleday, 1964.

Folsom, Marty. My dissertation and published articles can be found at martyfolsom.com/author

Grenz, Stanley J. *Created for Community: Connecting Christian Belief with Christian Living*. Grand Rapids: Baker Academic, 1998.

Gunton, Colin. *Enlightenment and Alienation: An Essay towards a Trinitarian Theology*. Grand Rapids: Eerdmans, 1985.

———. *The One, the Three and the Many: God, Creation, and the Culture of Modernity*. Cambridge: Cambridge University Press, 1993.

Jinkins, Michael. *Invitation to Theology*. Downers Grove: InterVarsity, 2001.

Kuhn, Thomas. *The Structure of Scientific Revolution*. Chicago: University of Chicago Press, 1962.

Larson, Bruce. *No Longer Strangers*. Waco: Word, 1971.

———. *The Relational Revolution*. Waco: Word, 1978.

Manning, Brennan. *Lion and Lamb: The Relentless Tenderness of Jesus*. Old Tappan, NJ: Revell, 1986.

Macmurray, John. *Freedom in the Modern World*. London: Faber & Faber, 1941.

Further Reading

————. *Persons in Relation*. New York: Harper, 1961.

————. *The Self as Agent*. London: Faber & Faber, 1957.

Newbigin, Lesslie. *Foolishness to the Greeks: The Gospel and Western Culture*. Grand Rapids: Eerdmans, 1986.

————. *The Gospel in a Pluralist Society*. Grand Rapids: Eerdmans, 1989.

Polanyi, Michael. *Personal Knowledge: Toward a Post-Critical Philosophy*. Chicago: University of Chicago Press, 1958.

Richardson, Ronald W. *Creating a Healthier Church: Family Systems Theory, Leadership, and Congregational Life*. Minneapolis: Augsburg Fortress, 1996.

Schaef, Anne Wilson. *The Addictive Organization*. San Francisco: HarperCollins, 1988.

Smail, Thomas. *The Forgotten Father: Rediscovering the Heart of the Christian Gospel*. London: Paternoster Press, 1980. Reprinted by Wipf & Stock Publishers, 2001.

Suttie, Ian. *The Origins of Love and Hate*. Mitcham, Victoria: Penguin, 1960.

Torrance, Alan. *Persons in Communion: An Essay on Trinitarian Description and Human Participation*. Edinburgh: T & T Clark, 1996.

Torrance, James. *Worship, Community & the Triune God of Grace*. Downer's Grove: InterVarsity, 1997.

Vanhoozer, Kevin. *Remythologizing Theology: Divine Action, Passion, and Authorship*. Cambridge: Cambridge University Press, 2012.

Wittgenstein, Ludwig. *Philosophical Investigations*. New York: John Wiley & Sons, 1953.